上海市职业教育"十四五"规划教材

职业教育国际商务专业教学用书

实用商务英语

主　编　朱红萍

华东师范大学出版社
·上海·

图书在版编目（CIP）数据

实用商务英语 / 朱红萍主编. — 上海：华东师范大学出版社，2023
ISBN 978-7-5760-3969-6

Ⅰ.①实… Ⅱ.①朱… Ⅲ.①商务—英语—职业教育—教材 Ⅳ.①F7

中国国家版本馆CIP数据核字（2023）第207893号

实用商务英语

主　　编　朱红萍
责任编辑　何　晶
审读编辑　袁一薳
责任校对　时东明　曹　勇
装帧设计　俞　越

出版发行　华东师范大学出版社
社　　址　上海市中山北路3663号　邮编 200062
网　　址　www.ecnupress.com.cn
电　　话　021-60821666　行政传真 021-62572105
客服电话　021-62865537　门市（邮购）电话 021-62869887
地　　址　上海市中山北路3663号华东师范大学校内先锋路口
网　　店　http://hdsdcbs.tmall.com

印 刷 者　上海景条印刷有限公司
开　　本　787毫米×1092毫米　1/16
印　　张　9.25
字　　数　196千字
版　　次　2023年12月第1版
印　　次　2023年12月第1次
书　　号　ISBN 978-7-5760-3969-6
定　　价　32.00元

出 版 人　王　焰

（如发现本版图书有印订质量问题，请寄回本社客服中心调换或电话021-62865537联系）

编委会

主　编：朱红萍

副主编：胡陈红　夏　莹

编　委：权冬欣　陈洁莉　朱敏斐　彭　丽
　　　　倪冰清　张玮琼　吴琪君

前言

时代风起云涌,电子商务、人工智能等新技术迅猛发展,新岗位新任务对人才培养提出了新要求。除了扎实的语言技能,职业学校商贸类专业的学生还需具备基本的商务知识和跨文化理解能力。在这样的时代背景下,编写一本既让学生感兴趣又能全面提高学生综合素养的商务英语教材也成为了"必然"。

为了激发学生学习兴趣,本教材的编写团队在充分的市场调研后,对初级商务工作进行了分类分层,对岗位的职业能力进行了提炼汇总,设置了层次分明的任务板块,为职业学校商务英语专业和其他商贸类专业的学生量身定制了这本商务英语基础教材。

本教材遵循情境教学法,按照实际的工作流程,把具体的工作任务分解成三个模块十个单元,囊括了"职场小白"进入职场后将要经历的各种典型商务场景,由浅入深、层次鲜明,职业能力要求螺旋上升。具体而言,本教材把日常商务工作分解成"了解公司""理解工作""懂点管理"三个模块,每个模块下设2—4个单元不等。在"Know Your Company(了解公司)"模块,学生将基本了解公司、职业、产品及客户的要素和特点;在"Understand Your Work(理解工作)"模块,学生将通过职场问候、接待客户、参加展会、销售产品等具体工作场景提升对商务活动的认知和理解;"Get to Know Management(懂点管理)"模块的要求进一步提高,学生将通过解决具体问题和分析描述图表对企业运营产生更完整和全面的认识。

本教材每个单元设有三个部分,每个部分都以工作任务为引领,涉及商务英语听、说、读、写以及综合运用等技能的培养与训练。值得一提的是,本教材尤其注重实用性和人文性的统一。一方面,突出语言的"交际性",有意识地提高学生商务英语听、说的实践量,除了Listening、Speaking、Scenario Speaking等听、说教学活动,还根据每单元的主题设计了十个Workshop,模拟真实商务情境,旨在使学生提升沟通合作能力和语言综合能力;另一方面,将课程思政要素有效融入教学目标与内容,在"润物细无声"中培养学生的爱国情怀和精益求精的职业精神,加强学生对中外文化异同的认识,提升其跨文化理解和沟通能力。

在此，特别要感谢为本教材提供支持和帮助的团队。首先，感谢与我一起共事的同事们，她们在从事商务英语教学和研究过程中积累的一线经验是本教材得以完成的重要基石；其次，感谢身处商务实战田野的企业专家，他们为教材的"适应性"提供了有利保障；最后，感谢在教材编写过程中提供了宝贵意见和建议的专家学者们。

朱红萍

2023年12月于上海

Contents

Module 1   Know Your Company

Unit 1	Companies	2
Unit 2	Occupations	12
Unit 3	Products	24
Unit 4	Customers	36

Module 2   Understand Your Work

Unit 5	Greetings	48
Unit 6	Meetings	60
Unit 7	Trade Fairs	72
Unit 8	Sales	84

Module 3   Get to Know Management

| Unit 9 | Troubleshooting | 100 |
| Unit 10 | Trends | 110 |

Appendix

Listening Scripts   124

Module 1 Know Your company

Unit 1 Companies

Learning Objectives:

On successful completion of this unit, you will be able to:
- request and provide general information on companies;
- discuss different industries and lines of business;
- explain the responsibilities of different departments;
- make a company profile.

company: a business organisation that makes, buys, or sells goods or provides services in exchange for money

Part 1   Introducing Companies

📖 Reading

Read the introduction of three multinational companies and guess their possible names.

1. _____

> Founded in Qingdao, China, in 1984, it has been dedicated to creating more values to users around the world, becoming a service provider to improve living environment. It has built 29 manufacturing bases, 8 research and development centres and 19 overseas trading companies around the world. The total number of its employees around the world reaches more than 60,000.

2. _____

> It was founded in 1987. It is a leading global provider of information and communications technology (ICT) infrastructure and smart devices. Its headquarters is located in Shenzhen, China. It has more than 194,000 employees, and operates in more than 170 countries and regions. Its mission is to bring digital to every person, home and organisation for a fully connected, intelligent world.

3. _____

> Since 1927, it has developed from a small local company to a famous multinational company. It has 70,330 employees worldwide and sales of $19,806 million. It manufactures cars, trucks, buses, and maritime and industrial engines. Its position as a major international group with large operations in Europe and North America is a result of quality, safety and caring for people and the environment. The headquarters is in Gothenburg, Sweden.

🔤 Language Focus

Study the following expressions for asking for and giving information on companies.

1. — When was the company founded?
   — It was founded in 1987.
   — Founded in 1984, it ....

2. — What does the company manufacture/provide?
   — It manufactures cars, trucks, buses, and maritime and industrial engines.
   — It is a provider of information and communications technology (ICT) infrastructure and smart devices.

Module 1 Know Your company

3. — Where is the headquarters?
   — Its headquarters is located in Shenzhen, China.
   — The headquarters is in Gothenburg, Sweden.
4. — How many employees does the company have?
   — It has more than 194,000 employees.
   — The total number of its employees around the world reaches more than 60,000.

Listening

Situation: There are three people introducing their companies.

Listen and complete the following profiles of the three companies.

1. Company A
   Nationality: _____
   Number of branches: _____
   Number of employees: _____

2. Company B
   Nationality: _____
   Head office: _____
   Number of dealerships: _____

3. Company C
   Nationality: _____
   Year of establishment: _____
   Number of employees: _____

Scenario Speaking

Imagine you and your partner work in ideal companies after graduation. Find out about your partner's ideal company by using the following sentence patterns and tell some other students about your partner's ideal company.

Questions	Answers
Who do you work for?	I work for ....

(Continued)

Questions	Answers
Is it a Chinese company?	Yes. It's a Chinese company. No. It's a British/American/... company.
Where is the headquarters?	Its headquarters is in ....
How many employees does your company have?	It has more than ... employees.
What does the company manufacture/provide?	It manufactares cars, trucks, buses, and maritime and industrial engines/provides information and communications technology (ICT) infrastructure and smart devices/....
Does your company have any branches/subsidiaries/offices/plants?	Yes. It has branches/subsidiaries/offices/plants in more than ... countries and regions/all over the world. No. It doesn't have any branches/subsidiaries/offices/plants.

Part 2 Talking about Lines of Business

📖 Reading

I. The following are three main types of industries. Read and study what they are.

Primary industry: It involves acquiring raw materials, which can be the mining of metals and coal, oil production, rubber extraction, agriculture industry, fisheries, etc. It is sometimes known as extractive industry.

Secondary industry: It includes manufacturing and assembling finished products. It involves converting raw materials into components, for example, making plastics from oil. It also involves assembling products, e.g. building houses, bridges and roads.

Tertiary industry: It refers to the commercial services that support the production and distribution, including insurance, transport, warehousing and other services, such as teaching and health care.

II. Study the following lines of business and tell which industry each belongs to.

fishing   _____
car making   _____
banking   _____
farming   _____
flour milling   _____
retailing   _____
restaurants   _____
mining   _____

🎧 Listening

Situation: There are six people introducing their companies.

I. Listen and match the names of the companies with their lines of business respectively.

1. Xiaomi •   • logistics

2. IKEA •   • consumer electronics

3. FedEx •   • newspaper reporting

4. Heineken •   • furniture and home decor

5. BYD •   • automobile

6. China Daily •   • beer

II. Can you think of more examples of lines of business? Please write them down on the line below.

_____

💬 Speaking

Read the words and phrase in the box aloud and categorise them accordingly in the following table.

| computer | credit card | smartphone | television |
| cosmetics | insurance | medicine | loan |

Chemical Sector	Financial Sector	Electronics Sector

🔤 Language Focus

I. Study the following expressions about companies and their lines of business.

1. BYD makes/manufactures/sells automobiles.
2. Shell is in the oil business.
3. — What does Heineken make?
   — It manufactures beer.
4. — Does IKEA make clothing?
   — No, it doesn't.

II. Complete these questions with *do* or *does*.

1. What _____ your company produce?
2. _____ Microsoft make computers?
3. What _____ Ford and Nissan sell?
4. _____ Supor manufacture consumer electronics?

Part 3 Describing Departments

🎧 Listening

Situation: A receptionist is talking to three visitors.

Listen and match the visitors with the departments they are looking for.

1. Visitor 1 •   • Marketing

2. Visitor 2 •   • HR (Human Resources)

3. Visitor 3 •   • After-sales

🔤 Language Focus

I. Study the following expressions frequently used by receptionists.

1. If there's an issue with your paycheque, you can talk to ….

2. If you have a problem with a product, you can contact ….

II. Read out the introduction of typical departments in a company and answer the questions below. You can answer the questions by using the above sentence patterns.

1. An HR department is responsible for recruiting, hiring and training employees. It also handles employee issues. Therefore, if you work in a company and want to get some professional development, the HR department can assist you.

2. R&D refers to research and development. An R&D department keeps a company's products innovative and competitive. It is responsible for developing new products and improving existing ones.

3. A marketing department promotes a company's products or services. It is responsible for doing market research to understand customers' needs and organising marketing campaigns to raise market awareness. The goal of the marketing department is to get people interested in a product or service.

4. A sales department sells the company's products or services. It may sell to other businesses or individual customers. The goal of a sales department is to get people

to buy a product or service.

5. An accounting department tracks how the company's money is spent and received. It reports and records company's cash flow and also manages its payroll.

6. A customer service department interacts with the company's customers. It is responsible for handling customers' complaints.

Questions:

1. Which department is responsible for developing products?
   _____

2. Which department deals with money matters of a company?
   _____

3. Which department promotes a company's newest product?
   _____

4. Which department sells a company's products or services?
   _____

📖 Reading

Read the dialogue and discuss the following questions.

A: Welcome to our company. Nice to meet you.

B: Nice to meet you, too. I am honoured to work with you as an intern. Can you tell me something about your company?

A: No problem. Our company is one of the world's top 500 enterprises. The company has good facilities and working environment, and the main lines of business are clothing trade and transportation.

B: What departments are there in the company?

A: Our company mainly has Human Resources Department, Marketing Department and R&D Department.

B: What is each department responsible for?

A: The Human Resources Department deals with staff issues, like salary, recruitment, and career development. The Marketing Department is responsible for marketing, sales and promotions. The R&D Department is the key to the Design and Engineering Department, and they decide the soul of our products.

B: R&D is a very important department of the company! What do I need to have if I am going to work in this department?

A: You need to have a wealth of experience, and the relevant engineering and technical knowledge.

B: Thank you.

Questions:

1. What is the main business of the company?

   _____
   _____
   _____

2. What departments does the company mainly have?

   _____
   _____
   _____

3. What do you need to have if you want to work in the R&D department?

   _____
   _____
   _____

Scenario Speaking

Imagine you are working for a company. Describe your responsibilities at work to your partner and let him/her guess which department you work in.

> **Example:**
>
> **Student A:** I have a lot of contact with customers because they often phone us when they have problems with our machines, which is quite often. They phone us because they need spare parts — something's broken or worn out — and then I take the orders and send parts to the customers.
>
> **Student B:** You must work in the after-sales department.

Unit 1 Companies

🏛 Workshop

Work in groups of three to four to complete the following task. Suppose you and the group members are going to set up a new company. Study the following example and work out your plan.

	Example	Your company
Name	B. S. World Co., Ltd	
Logo	暗香	
Location	No.918 Lujiabang Road, Huangpu District, Shanghai, China	
Line of business	Secondary industry	
Products or services	Sachet	
Departments	Business Unit 1 Business Unit 2 Administration Department Human Resources Department Finance Department	

📝 Self-evaluation Checklist

	Assessment criteria	Competent	Not yet competent
Part 1 Introducing companies	1. Be able to retell key information on a company		
	2. Be able to introduce the name, location, and main business of a company		
Part 2 Talking about lines of business	1. Be able to understand what the three main types of industries are		
	2. Be able to identify the lines of business of various companies		
Part 3 Describing the departments of a company	1. Be able to tell the names of the departments of a company		
	2. Be able to identify the functions of the departments of a company		

Unit 2　Occupations

Learning Objectives:

On successful completion of this unit, you will be able to:
- discuss different types of jobs;
- describe job responsibilities;
- talk about ideal jobs;
- express likes and dislikes.

occupation: a person's usual or principal work or business

Part 1 Talking about Different Jobs

🎧 Listening (Dialogue)

I. **Warm-up:** Think and discuss what information a business card usually includes.

II. **Situation:** A receptionist is talking to a caller on the phone. He wants to find out who the caller wants to speak to, Robert Brown or George Braun.
Listen to the conversation. Then read the following business cards and tell who the caller wants to speak to.

Robert Brown ABC Technologies Co. Ltd.
Sales Manager
Sales Department

Address: Room 1401, No.XXX, Lujiabang Road, Huangpu District, Shanghai, China
Postcode: 518129
Tel: 86-21-88XXXX88-1235; 86-189-XXXX-6968
E-mail: rbrown@xxx.com
Website: www.xxxtechco.com

George Braun ABC Technologies Co. Ltd.
Software Engineer
Information Technology Department

Address: Room 1403, No.XXX, Lujiabang Road, Huangpu District, Shanghai, China
Postcode: 518129
Tel: 86-21-88XXXX88-3469; 86-189-XXXX-6869
E-mail: gbraun@xxx.com
Website: www.xxxtechco.com

🔤 Language Focus

I. Name the jobs in the six pictures below.

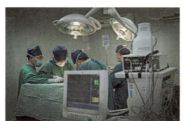

II. Here are some more words and phrases about jobs in the box. Read and put them under the correct headings.

| accountant | sales clerk | lawyer | CEO | engineer |
| marketing manager | receptionist | supervisor | assistant | |

Professional and technical	Administrative and managerial	Clerical and office

III. Please add one more job under each heading in the above table.

Listening (Passage)

Situation: An economist is talking about the workforce of a country. Listen and fill in the correct percentages on the chart.

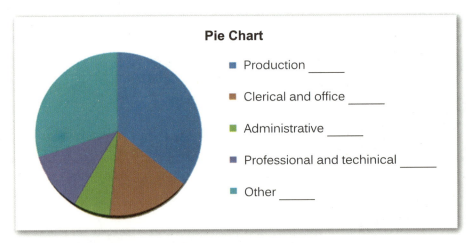

Pie Chart
- Production _____
- Clerical and office _____
- Administrative _____
- Professional and techinical _____
- Other _____

Scenario Speaking

I. Listen to the following words and mark the stress of each word by underlining the stressed syllables.

1. accountant (*n.*)
2. export (*n.*)

3. secretary (*n.*)
4. engineer (*n.*)
5. marketing (*n.*)

II. Do you like any of the professions or jobs listed in Part 1? If not, what professions, occupations or jobs do you like? Work in pairs to complete the following tasks. Talk about your favourite job with your partner by using the following sentence patterns. Then, tell other students about your partner's favourite job.

Questions	Answers
What work do you want to do?	I want to/would like to be ….
What's your favourite job/profession/occupation?	My favourite job/profession/occupation is a/an ….
Where do you want to work?	I want to work in ….

Part 2 Describing Job Duties

📖 Reading

Six people are introducing themselves. Read their self-introductions and write the correct names under the job titles below.

My name's John Wang. I help to make sure the company is producing what people want to buy, and also promote our products.

I'm David Asaad. I do the bookkeeping and the payroll.

I'm Maria Dawson. I'm responsible for recruitment and staff welfare issues.

Module 1 Know Your company

I'm Tim Zhang. I deal with our suppliers and make sure we buy equipment and materials at the best prices.

My name's Angelica Rosetti. My area of responsibility is planning and testing new products.

I'm Mark Jenkins. I'm responsible for computer systems. I install hardware and software and fix computer problems.

Job titles	HR Manager	Marketing Assistant	R&D Manager
Names	_____	_____	_____
Job titles	IT Support Engineer	Accountant	Purchasing Manager
Names	_____	_____	_____

🔤 Language Focus

Study the following expressions for asking for and giving information on job duties.

1. — What does she do?
   — She's a marketing assistant.
   — What does her job involve?
   — She helps to make sure the company is producing what people want to buy and promotes the products.

2. — What does he do?
   — He's a purchasing manager.
   — What does his job involve?
   — He deals with the suppliers and makes sure the company buys equipment and materials at the best prices.

 **Listening**

I. Match the following job titles with their job duties.

Job titles	Job duties
( ) 1. chief financial officer (CFO)	A. visits customers, leaves sample, sells products and supports the customer service department
( ) 2. management consultant	B. is responsible for testing new products and deals with customers' complaints
( ) 3. human resources manager	C. interviews clients and gives them advice
( ) 4. quality manager	D. is responsible for the company's accounts, and controls money coming in and going out
( ) 5. sales representative	E. recruits new employees and participates in evaluating the performance of staff

II. Situation: Five people are introducing themselves.
    Listen to their self-introduction and complete the following table.

	Names	Job titles	Job duties
1	Caroline Green		
2	Jan Nowak		
3	Kostas William		
4	Susan Ferguson		
5	Maria Salgado		

👥 Scenario Speaking

Imagine you and your partner both work in your ideal companies after graduation. Find out about your partner's job duties by using the following sentence patterns and tell other students about your partner's job duties.

Questions	Answers
What do you do?	I'm a management consultant/sales representative/....
What does your job involve?	I interview clients and give them advice/visit customers and sell products/....

Part 3   Talking about Ideal Jobs

💬 Speaking

I. Some people are talking about their likes about their jobs. Read and discuss which of the following conditions you would prefer. Please give your reasons.

an encouraging boss

safe working environment

flexible working hours

professional development

good team spirit

a sense of accomplishments

long holidays

short daily commute

extra benefits

II. Work in pairs to complete the following task. Think and discuss the questions below.

Generally speaking, which conditions are usually important for:

1. someone who wants to make a fortune?
2. someone with a family?
3. someone with a clear professional development plan?
4. someone who wants work-and-life balance?

Listening

I. Read the following list of items connected with work. Mark them in the following table by using √, × and —.

√ = the factor that you think is important and that satisfies you now;

× = the factor that you don't think is important and that doesn't satisfy you now;

— = the factor that you don't have an opinion on or you don't feel strongly about now.

	You	1. Nancy	2. John	3. Tom
Boss				
Colleague				
Working hour				
Holiday				
Salary				
Commuting				

II. Situation: Three people are talking about their jobs respectively.

Listen and fill in the above table in the same way that you have done for yourself.

📝 Language Focus

I. Study the following expressions for describing likes and dislikes.

1. Describing likes:
   - like + doing sth.
   - love + doing sth.
   - enjoy + doing sth.
   - prefer + doing sth.
   - be fond of + doing sth.
   - be keen on + doing sth.
   - be interested in + doing sth.
   - I think it's wonderful/delightful/... to do sth.

2. Describing dislikes:
   - don't like + doing sth.
   - dislike + doing sth.
   - hate + doing sth.
   - don't care for + doing sth.
   - can't bear + doing sth.
   - can't stand + doing sth.
   - I think it's terrible/dull/disgusting/... to do sth.

II. Complete these sentences according to your likes and dislikes about jobs.

1. I _____ having a high salary.
2. I _____ to have a long holiday.
3. I _____ spending a long time commuting to work.
4. I _____ working with friendly colleagues.
5. I _____ having a terrific boss.

III. Think about two more things you like and you don't like about jobs. Then compare your answers with your partner. What is similar and what is different?

_____
_____
_____
_____

👥 Scenario Speaking

Talk about your ideal job with your partner by using the following sentence patterns.

Questions	Answers
What is your ideal job?	My ideal job is ....
What are the duties of the job? (List at least three duties.)	My ideal job involves many duties, such as ....
Why do you like this job?	Because ....

🏛 Workshop

Based on the achievement you have got in the workshop of Unit 1, continue to work on the plan for your new company.

Please pay attention to the following questions:

- How many staff are you going to employ for each department?
- What are the major responsibilities of each department?

Study the following example of B. S. World Co., Ltd and finish your plan.

Department	No. of staff	Major responsibilities
Business Unit 1 & 2	18	It is a comprehensive department including purchasing department, marketing department and sales department.
Administration Department	3	It is mainly responsible for organising meetings, writing meeting minutes and communicating with all members of the company. It also needs to write business letters to other practice firms in the world.
Human Resources Department	4	It is responsible for the attendance sheet, making a payroll for employees and also organising company's training, drafting the employment contract, etc.
Finance Department	3	It is responsible for making a financial statement, invoice form, bookkeeping voucher and online payment. It needs to check the bank statement every day.

Your plan

Department	No. of staff	Major responsibilities

📋 Self-evaluation Checklist

	Assessment criteria	Competent	Not yet competent
Part 1 **Talking about different jobs**	1. Be able to read business cards		
	2. Be able to identify different types of jobs		
Part 2 **Describing job duties**	1. Be able to understand major job duties and responsibilities of common jobs		
	2. Be able to describe job duties and responsibilities		
Part 3 **Talking about ideal jobs**	1. Be able to express likes and dislikes about jobs		
	2. Be able to describe and talk about ideal jobs		

Unit 3 Products

Learning Objectives:

On successful completion of this unit, you will be able to:

- discuss different types of products;
- describe the features of products;
- compare different products;
- choose the right products for the company.

product: something produced and sold in large quantities, often as a result of a manufacturing process

Unit 3   Products   **25**

Part 1   Talking about Different Types of Products

💬 Speaking

A type of products means a group that products belong to, such as household products, cosmetics, baby products, and so on. Look at the following products and choose the right type for each of them.

A   B   C

(   ) 1. electronic devices   (   ) 2. furniture   (   ) 3. cosmetics

🔤 Language Focus

I. Study the following expressions for talking about the types of goods.

1. This product belongs to ….
2. This is a … product.

II. Categorise the following products and talk to your partner about them.

> **Example:**
> This product belongs to **household goods**. /This is a household product.

food jar

lipstick

headphone

moisturizing cream

bookcase

digital camera

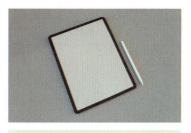 tablet

 blender

 mascara

 cabinet

 sofa

 blue-tooth speaker

Electronic devices	Cosmetics	Household goods

Listening

Situation: Verona Adam is going to talk about two types of products: *fast-moving consumer goods* (FMCG) and *consumer durables.*

Listen to the presentation and decide whether the following statements are True or False.

(　　) 1. Shoes are consumer durables.

(　　) 2. Canned drinks belong to consumer durables.

(　　) 3. Milk and vegetables should be categorised into fast-moving consumer goods.

(　　) 4. Washing machines are fast-moving consumer goods.

(　　) 5. Envelopes belong to consumer durables.

Scenario Speaking

Suppose you and your partner are preparing to furnish the new office with a fund of $5,000. The following table contains the products available at the moment. Work in pairs to complete the following task. Discuss and decide with your partner what products you are going to buy.

	Office furniture & office equipment		
	Table	Telephone	Seating
Office supplies plus	office table $100	standard $100	armchair $100
	reception table ... $100	with answering machine $250	sofa $450
		cordless $300	
	Storage	Computer	Lamp
	filing cabinet $300	notebook $1,500	table lamp $50
	cupboard $250	desktop $1,000	LED lamp $70

Part 2   Describing Products

📖 Reading

Look at the following products and match each one with its correct description.

 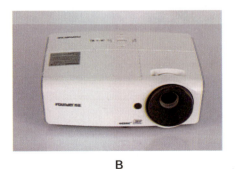  

　　A　　　　　　　　B　　　　　　　　C　　　　　　　　D

(   ) 1. It is a rectangular container with a hard frame and a handle, used to carry clothes and possessions while travelling.

(   ) 2. It is a machine that makes a film or other images appear on a screen or other surfaces by using light through a lens.

(   ) 3. It is a wooden piece of furniture with two or three doors. You use it to keep documents in.

Module 1 Know Your company

(   ) 4. It is made up of a piece of plastic on a stand. You use it to hold large pieces of paper when you give a talk.

🔤 Language Focus

I. Study the following expressions for asking and answering about product features.

1. — What colour is it?
   — It's yellow.
2. — What is it made of?
   — It's made of cotton.
3. — What is its shape?
   — It's a circle.
4. — How do you like the product?
   — It's elegant.
5. — What do you use it for?
   — We use it to keep the office cool.

II. Write down more expressions to describe product features.

Material	Shape	Personal feeling
cotton	round	comfortable

🎧 Listening

Situation: A salesperson is making a presentation about the new videophone. Listen to the presentation and choose the best answer.

1. The name of the product is _____.
   A. ViTa Desktop Videophone

B. ViaTV Desktop Videophone

   C. Via Desktop Videophone

2. The salesperson describes the product as _____.

   A. small and slim

   B. small and attractive

   C. small and elegant

3. To set up the product you need _____.

   A. a touch-tone phone

   B. a computer

   C. special software

4. The special feature that the salesperson does not mention is _____.

   A. full colour motion video

   B. on-screen menus

   C. very good picture quality

5. In order to see the person you are calling, _____.

   A. only you need the product

   B. only the receiver needs the product

   C. both parties need the product

Scenario Speaking

Suppose you and your partner work for a company that makes bags. Work in pairs to complete the following task. Think and discuss about the features of the bags produced by your company. Then make an oral presentation about your products. You can refer to the tips on *How to give a presentation*.

The details of the following should be included:

- name
- size
- materials
- colour
- shape
- function

How to give a presentation

1. **Greet and introduce yourself**
   Ladies and gentlemen, it is an honour to address such a distinguished audience. My name is ....
   Good morning/afternoon. My name is ....

2. **Introduce your presentation**
   I'd like to talk about ....
   The purpose of this presentation is to ....

3. **Show how many parts there are in your presentation**
   There are three sections in my presentation. They are ....
   My presentation is made up of three parts.

4. **Link your parts**
   Firstly, I'd like to tell you about ....
   Secondly, I will talk about ....
   Let's turn to the last point. It is about ....

5. **Make a conclusion**
   To sum up, ...
   In conclusion, we need to ....

Part 3   Comparing Products

Reading

Read the information about Desk A and Desk B. Then, decide whether the following statements are True or False. If a statement is false, correct it.

Desk A
- 1.2 metres long, 0.8 metre wide
- About 50 KG
- Free 24-hour delivery
- 14-day money-back guarantee
- Maintenance support by telephone hotline during business hours

Unit 3　Products　**31**

Desk B
- 1.5 metres long, 1 metre wide
- About 80 KG
- 48-hour delivery
- 7-day money-back guarantee
- Maintenance at the factory

(　) 1. Desk A is cheaper than Desk B.
_____

(　) 2. Desk B is longer than Desk A.
_____

(　) 3. Desk A has a longer delivery time than Desk B.
_____

(　) 4. Desk B has better maintenance support than Desk A.
_____

(　) 5. Desk A has a longer money-back guarantee.
_____

🔤 Language Focus

I. Study the following expressions for comparing products.

1. The desktop is **cheaper than** the notebook.
   The notebook is **more expensive than** the desktop.
2. It is **the best** seller.
3. The notebook's warranty is **as long as** the desktop's.
   The notebook is **not as good as** the desktop.

II. Now use the prompts to make sentences. Add additional words if necessary.

1. pen/than/more expensive/pencil
_____
_____

2. spend/time/longer/I/going to the library/going to the park/than
_____
_____

3. bought/a cap/as good as/he/his father's

_____
_____

 Listening

Situation: A man wants to purchase a new watch. He is calling a shop assistant.

Listen to the conversation and fill in the details in the table below.

	Model A	Model B
New function		
Price		
Warranty		
Service		
Money-back guarantee		
Delivery		

Scenario Speaking

Suppose you are going to purchase a printer for your company. Work in pairs to complete the following task. Make a dialogue to compare the two printers and decide which printer to buy according to the information list.

	Printer CG566	Printer DF432
Size	380×293×211 (mm)	364×247×190 (mm)
Price	￥1,649	￥999
Speed	20 pages per min	22 pages per min
Weight	6.95 KG	4.7 KG
Photo print	no	yes
Delivery	in stock	in 1 week

Workshop

Based on the achievement you have got in the workshops of Unit 1 and Unit 2, think what product you want to sell. You can refer to the useful expressions below.

You are required to:

- describe the product;
- compare your product with other similar products on the market;
- make an oral report to introduce your product.

The following details should be included:

Describe the product	name, size, weight, colour, features, ...
Compare the products	similarities
	differences

Useful Expressions

Our product is called ....
It is ... long, ... wide and ... high.
It weighs ....
It can be used to ....
Compared with ..., our product has ....
It is ... than ....

Self-evaluation Checklist

	Assessment criteria	Competent	Not yet competent
Part 1 Talking about different types of products	1. Be able to talk about the types of products		
	2. Be able to classify different types of products		
Part 2 Describing products	1. Be able to notice different aspects to describe the products		
	2. Be able to describe the features of products		
Part 3 Comparing products	1. Be able to tell the differences between products		
	2. Be able to compare different products and choose the right products for the company		

Unit 4 Customers

Learning Objectives:

On successful completion of this unit, you will be able to:
- write letters to establish a business relation;
- make and reply to an offer;
- deal with a complaint.

customer: a person or an organisation that buys something from a shop or business

Part 1 Establishing Business Relations

📖 Reading

I. Warm-up: Think and discuss the following questions.

1. What are the possible ways of knowing customers?
2. If you hope to establish business ties with potential customers, what should you do?

II. Read the following two letters and think what the aims of these two letters are.

Letter 1

Dear Wang Qiang,

   We owed your name and address to your booth in China International Trade Fair. Your staff have shown us your various products.

   We are writing in the hope of establishing business relations with you.

   At present, we are interested in possibly purchasing silk blouses and would be grateful if you could send us your catalogue and all necessary information on the above goods.

   Should your price be found competitive, we intend to place an order with you.

   We look forward to receiving your early reply.

Yours sincerely,

Grace Perez

Grace Perez (Ms.)
Purchasing Manager
Fashion Trading Co., Ltd

Letter 2

Dear Ms. Perez,

   Thank you for your letter of 25 October saying that you intend to establish direct business connections with us, which happens to be our desire.

   We are a state-owned corporation, handling both the import and export of garments. In order to acquaint you with our business lines, we enclose a copy of our Export List covering the goods and information you require at present.

   It is our policy to trade with merchants of various countries on the basis of equality, mutual benefit and exchange of needed goods. We hope to promote, through mutual efforts, both trade and friendship.

　　　Your early reply will be highly appreciated.

Yours sincerely,

Wang Qiang

Wang Qiang

Sales Manager

China National Garments Imp. & Exp. Corporation

💬 Speaking

According to the information provided in Part 1 Reading, answer the following questions.

1. How does Grace Perez know about the company which sells silk blouses?
2. What does Grace Perez enquire about in her letter?
3. How does Wang Qiang acknowledge the receipt of a letter?
4. Does Wang Qiang introduce his company?

🔤 Language Focus

Study the following expressions for writing letters to establish business relations. Pay attention to the writing steps.

1. **Show the source of information:**
    a. We owed your name and address to your booth in China International Import Expo.
    b. We learned your name and address from the Commercial Counsellor's Office of the British Embassy in Beijing.

2. **State the purpose of the letter:**
    a. We are writing to establish business relations with you.
    b. We are writing to cooperate with you.

3. **Make an enquiry:**
    a. We are interested in possibly purchasing silk blouses and would be grateful if you could send us your catalogue and all necessary information on the above goods.
    b. It would be appreciated if you could send us some brochures and samples.

4. **Acknowledge the receipt of the letter:**
    a. Thank you for your letter of 25 October saying that you intend to establish direct business connections with us, which happens to be our desire.
    b. I am writing to tell you that I have received your letter of 25 October saying that you would like to establish business ties with us.

5. **Make a company introduction:**
   a. We are a state-owned corporation, handling both the import and export business of garments.
   b. Our lines are mainly in clothing industry.

✎ Scenario Writing

I. **Suppose you are a purchasing manager working in Shanghai Sports Shoes Co., Ltd. You know a supplier (Fabre Trading Co., Ltd) from an advertisement in *Fashion Magazine*. You would like to buy some products from this supplier. Write a letter to the supplier.**

You are required to:

- show the source of information;
- state the purpose of your letter;
- make an enquiry.

II. **Now suppose you are the sales manager in Fabre Trading Co., Ltd. You have recently received a letter from Shanghai Sports Shoes Co., Ltd., which wants to import some products from your company. Reply to this letter.**

You are required to:

- acknowledge the receipt of the letter;
- introduce your company;
- express the desire to establish business relations.

Part 2 Making Offers

🎧 Listening (Dialogue 1)

Situation: A secretary is making offers to three customers respectively.

I. Listen and match each offer with the customer's reply.

Offers	Replies
(　) 1. I can give you an earlier appointment, if you like.	A. Thank you very much. That would be very nice.
(　) 2. Would you like a cup of coffee?	B. That's very kind of you, but I think I'll walk and get some exercise.
(　) 3. Shall I call a taxi for you?	C. Yes, that would be very helpful. Thank you.

II. Listen again and answer the following questions.

1. What does the secretary offer to do in each conversation?
2. Does the customer accept or decline the offer in each conversation?

🔤 Language Focus

Study the following expressions for making an offer and replying to an offer.

1. **Making an offer:**
    a. Do you want me to get you a taxi?
    b. I can give you an earlier appointment, if you like.
    c. Shall I book you a hotel?

2. **Accepting an offer:**
    a. Thank you. That's very kind of you.
    b. Yes, please, if it's no trouble.
    c. Thank you very much. That would be very nice.

3. **Declining an offer:**
    a. No. Don't worry.
    b. It's all right. Thank you.
    c. That's very kind of you, but I think ....

Listening (Dialogue 2)

Situation: Sarah phones Terry, but he is not in. Kevin is answering the phone and taking a message.

Listen to the conversation and fill in the missing information in Kevin's message.

> From: Sarah
> To: Terry
> Date: 16 October, 2023
> Time: 14:35
>
> Message:
> She is arriving _____.
> She is travelling to downtown by _____ from Shanghai Pudong International Airport.
>
> To do:
> reserve a table for _____
> leave her a message about _____
> send her _____

Scenario Speaking

Work in pairs to complete the following task. Make a dialogue according to the directions.

Situation:

Sam works in Shanghai office of an international marketing company. A customer, Sally, who comes from the USA, is visiting his office. Sam has been asked to help Sally organise her visit.

Roles:

Student A: Sam

Student B: Sally

Requirements:

You are required to include in your dialogue whether Sally:

1. needs to go somewhere;

2. wants to go to a concert;

3. wants to go to a restaurant;

4. wants to go to her hotel;

5. wants to go on a tour;

6. wants information about the timetable for trains.

Part 3 Dealing with Complaints

📖 Reading

Read this article about telephone etiquette and fill in the missing information with the following sentences.

A. Here's how we handle that. Please call or write to ….

B. I'll see what I can do.

C. May I help you?

D. Never begin your sentences with a negative word.

E. I will just check for you.

We often have telephone conversations with our customers and it is important that we pay attention to the way we talk or "behave" over phone. Professionalism means to be polite, thoughtful, efficient, educated and provide valuable information at all times. If we want to make the first impression a good one, the following five phrases should be forbidden.

1. "What's wrong?"
   Say "_____" instead.
2. "I don't know."
   Replace this with "_____"
3. "We don't do that."
   Try to offer an alternative or say: "_____"
4. "You must …."
   It must not be used. Tell the customer what needs to be done by saying: "_____"
5. "No …."
   Remember: _____

🎧 Listening

Situation: Susan Sun from High Technology is phoning Mr. Pan, a supplier.

I. Listen to the conversation and check whether Mr. Pan's notes are correct. Then find out what Susan's complaint is.

From: Susan Sun
             High Technology

Module 1 Know Your company

> 6456 5063
>
> Order No. CEM1758 for TAE50 and TBC15. Placed the order two weeks ago and hasn't received TBC15 yet. Needs it by the end of the month. Phone back.

II. Listen again and answer the following question.

(   ) Which of the following reasons does Mr. Pan give for the delay?

    A. Problems in the production department.

    B. Problems at the supplier's factory.

    C. Problems with the shipping company.

🔤 Language Focus

I. Study the following expressions for making a complaint and dealing with a complaint.

1. Explaining the complaint:

    a. It seems you sent the wrong products.

    b. We ordered a computer but we received a printer.

2. Asking for more details:

    a. Would you please tell me your order number?

    b. Could I have the order number?

3. Giving information:

    a. Let me see. It's CEM1758.

    b. Let's see. It's 637816.

4. Explaining what has caused the complaint:

    a. I'm very sorry. There's been a delay with the computers.

    b. I'm terribly sorry. We've had problems with our manufacturer.

5. Asking when the goods can be delivered:

    a. When can I expect the delivery?

    b. When will you deliver the goods?

6. Apologising and saying what you will do:

    a. I'm very sorry. I'll see what I can do.

    b. I'm sorry. I'll check it for you.

II. Read the above sentences aloud in pairs.

Scenario Speaking

Work in pairs to complete the following task. Make a dialogue according to the directions.

Situation:

Two weeks ago Ada placed an order of 15 phone cases with DBC Gifts. She received the package this morning. When Ada opened it, she found 15 pencil cases, so she is going to phone DBC Gifts and complain about the problem. Peter works for the After-sales Department in DBC Gifts.

The following table shows the specific information about Ada's order.

Order No.: CFA3568		
Description	Quantity	Unit price
D2965 Phone cases	15	￥20
		Total: ￥300

The following is part of Peter's catalogue.

	Description	Price
D2965	Phone cases	￥20
D2956	Pencil cases	￥18

Roles:

Student A: Ada

Student B: Peter

Requirements:

Your dialogue should include the following contents:

1. Ada phones to complain about a delivery;
2. Peter finds out what the problem is and deals with the complaint.

🏛 Workshop

Suppose you are a trainer in MVP Trade Co., Ltd. You are going to give a presentation to the new employees on the tips of dealing with customers. Work in groups of three to four to complete the following task. Discuss what tips to be included in your presentation.

You are required to:

- Discuss from the following aspects:

    a. writing letters to establish business relations;

    b. replying to offers;

    c. dealing with complaints.

- Choose one aspect and give the presentation to the class.

📄 Self-evaluation Checklist

	Assessment criteria	Competent	Not yet competent
Part 1 Establishing business relations	1. Be able to state the writing steps of establishing business relations		
	2. Be able to write letters to establish business relations		
Part 2 Making offers	1. Be able to make an offer		
	2. Be able to reply to an offer		
Part 3 Dealing with complaints	1. Be able to make a complaint		
	2. Be able to deal with a complaint		

Module 2
Understand Your Work

Unit 5　Greetings

Learning Objectives:

On successful completion of this unit, you will be able to:

- introduce yourself and others;
- identify yourself and others;
- talk about business etiquette;
- make small talks with business partners.

> **greeting:** something polite or friendly that you say or do when you meet someone

Part 1   Introducing Yourself and Others

💬 Speaking

Match the questions with the responses. Then work in pairs to read the dialogue.

(   ) 1. I'm sorry. What's your name again?   A. I work for ABC Co. as an accountant.

(   ) 2. What do people call you?   B. I'm from Brazil.

(   ) 3. How do you spell your last name?   C. Everyone calls me Beth.

(   ) 4. Where are you from?   D. It's Elizabeth Silva.

(   ) 5. Who do you work for?   E. S-I-L-V-A.

🎧 Listening

Situation: David and Lily are introducing themselves.

I. Listen to their conversation and complete the missing information.

David: Hello, I'm David White. I'm _____ here.

Lily: Hi. My name is Lily Collins, but _____ Lily.

David: OK. Where are you from, Lily?

Lily: I'm from America. How _____?

David: _____ Mexico.

Lily: Oh, I love Mexico! It's really beautiful.

David: Thanks. _____ America.

II. Listen to the conversation again and read the dialogue with your partner.

🔤 Language Focus

I. Study the following expressions for introducing others.

1. Introducing other people:

   a. This is ....   b. I'd like to introduce ....

   c. Do you know ...?   d. Have you met ...?

2. Giving information about other people:

   a. She's from ....   b. He works in ....

II. Complete the conversation with the sentences in the box.

> A. Cream and sugar, please.
> B. Pleased to meet you, Mr. Toncini.
> C. He works in Milan.
> D. Have a seat, Giovanni.
> E. How are things?
> F. do you know Brian Turner,

Alice: Hello, Giovanni. Good to see you again. (1) _____
Giovanni: Just fine. And you?
Alice: Oh, not too bad. Giovanni, (2) _____ our new Personnel Manager? Brian, this is Giovanni Toncini. He's from Italy. (3) _____
Brian: (4) _____
Giovanni: Please, call me Giovanni.
Brian: And I'm Brian.
Alice: (5) _____
Giovanni: Thank you.
Alice: How about some coffee, Giovanni?
Giovanni: Yes, please. (6) _____

III. Now listen to the conversation and check your answers.

👥 Scenario Speaking

Work in groups of three to complete the following task. Make a dialogue according to the directions.

Situation:
Ms./Mr. Wu works for SK Light in Shanghai, Ms./Mr. Smith works for Bank of Shanghai in Hong Kong SAR, and Ms./Mr. Li works for Infotech Computing in Beijing. They are introducing themselves and others.

Roles:
Student A: Ms./Mr. Wu
Student B: Ms./Mr. Smith
Student C: Ms./Mr. Li

Requirements:
Please get to know each other by taking turns.

Part 2 Identifying Yourself and Others

📖 Reading

Representatives from two companies are going to discuss their transaction, and the first thing they do is to identify themselves. Read the sentences 1-4 and match them with the proper responses A-D.

(　) 1. I'm very pleased to meet you, Mr. Black.

(　) 2. You must be Jet. It's good to meet you at last.

(　) 3. We're especially pleased that our CEO, Charles, has flown from New York just to be with us.

(　) 4. Perhaps you'd like to take us through today's agenda.

A. Yes, I'm Jet. And it's a pleasure to meet you, too, Ms. Morrison.

B. Certainly, let's go through it.

C. Charles, please. And I'm thrilled to meet you, Mr. Smith.

D. Thank you, I'm really glad to be involved.

📖 Reading

I. Read the passage about reception desk etiquette and match the headings with the paragraphs.

A. Desk appearance

B. Greeting

C. Welcoming etiquette

D. Personal manner

Reception Desk Etiquette

If you are sitting behind a reception desk, you are the first person to interact with a visitor, and you can set the tone for the visit. You can give a visitor a great first impression or annoy him/her so much that he/she complains about you to the person he/she comes to see. All visitors should be welcomed warmly. The visitor isn't interrupting your business; the visitor IS your business.

_____

Look up and smile when someone approaches your desk. If you are on a personal call, hang up immediately. If you are on a business call, make eye contact with the visitor to indicate that you see him/her and will be with him/her shortly. As soon as you have finished your phone call, focus on the visitor with a smile. Apologise for the delay. Ask how you can help. Put warmth into the question, so it doesn't seem offhand.

_____

Ask the visitor if he/she would like to have a seat while you contact the person referred to. Depending on your company's policy, offer coffee or tea or direct the visitor to the coffee room. Offer to hang up his/her coat or show where it can be hung. Call the person who will be meeting the visitor. Use Ms. or Mr. when addressing the visitor.

_____

Besides smiling, modulate your voice. Be aware that you can convey what you think by the tone of your voice.

_____

Don't eat at your desk. If you can't avoid it, choose food that doesn't have a lingering aroma. In other words, no pizza or spaghetti. Keep a clean desk, even if you have other tasks to do besides dealing with visitors.

II. Answer the following questions.

1. Generally speaking, who will meet the visitor first in the company?
   _____

2. What should you do when a visitor arrives while you are having a business call?
   _____
   _____
   _____

3. When receiving a visitor, how do you show a good company image?
   _____
   _____
   _____
   _____

📇 Language Focus

I. Study the following expressions for identifying yourself and others.

	Identifying yourself	Identifying others
Name	• My name is .... • I am	• May I have your name, sir? • What's your name please?
Company/ Title	• I come from ABC Company. • I work for ABC Company as	• May I ask which company you come from? • Are you ... (name) from ...?
Purpose	• I'd like to talk to him about .... • I want to discuss ... with	• Is there anything particular you want to talk about? • Do you have an appointment with ...?

II. Fill in each blank in the following dialogue with a proper phrase or sentence according to the above expressions.

Visitor: Is this Mr. Smith's office?

Receptionist: Yes, that's right. What can I do for you?

Visitor: I'd like to see Mr. Smith, but I haven't got an appointment, I'm afraid.

Receptionist: Mr. Smith is engaged at present. _____?

Visitor: My name is Sam Williams.

Receptionist: _____?

Visitor: I come from ABC Company.

Receptionist: And is there _____?

Visitor: Yes, I'd like to talk to him about a new product our firm has recently launched.

Receptionist: I'm sorry, Mr. Williams. I'm afraid Mr. Smith can't see you today. He's in a meeting at the moment. You can leave your card here. Perhaps he can arrange a future appointment with you.

Visitor: All right. Thank you.

Receptionist: You are welcome.

III. Listen to the dialogue and practise it with your partner.

IV. From the above dialogue, find out words and phrases similar in meaning to the following.

1. item _____
2. company _____
3. release _____
4. conference _____
5. be busy doing sth. _____
6. make an arrangement _____

Scenario Speaking

Work in pairs to complete the following task. Make a dialogue according to the directions.

Situation:

The assistant to the General Manager is going to pick up a potential customer, Mr. Williams, at the airport. He has just arrived in Shanghai from New York. It is the first time for them to meet.

Roles:

Student A: the assistant

Student B: Mr. Williams

Requirements:

You are required to include the following content in your dialogue:

1. greeting and identifying each other;
2. offering help with the luggage;
3. taking Mr. Williams to the taxi.

Part 3   Making Small Talks

Speaking

I. Look at the pictures of different greetings around the world and answer the following questions.

1. Where do you think people greet each other in the ways shown in the pictures respectively?
2. Do you know any other ways of greeting people in the world?

II. Read these topics you might talk about when socialising with an English-speaking visitor you don't know very well. Put a tick (√) next to five most appropriate topics, and a cross (×) to five least appropriate topics.

☐ art   ☐ money   ☐ drink
☐ business   ☐ marriage   ☐ hobbies and interests
☐ political figures ☐ movies   ☐ racial tension
☐ fashion   ☐ sport   ☐ holidays
☐ food   ☐ religion   ☐ weather

III. When business people meet for the first time, what do they usually do? Discuss with your partner and put a tick (√) next to your answers.

☐ Shake hands.
☐ Exchange business cards.
☐ Bow to each other.
☐ Get down to business right away.
☐ Have dinner together after a talk.
☐ Talk about a neutral subject (such as trip) before getting down to business.

Listening

Situation: Business people usually have small talks on different topics before they get down to business.

Listen to the sentences on small talk topics and fill in the missing information.

Small talk

1. The woman drinks _____ _____.
2. The man's company is opening a _____ _____ in Britain.
3. The little girl has started school and in the _____ year now.
4. The little girl likes school. It's much more fun than _____ _____ _____.

Talks on cities

1. In the man's impression, the woman's city is clean, _____ and _____.
2. The man really admires the city's long history and _____ _____.
3. The best time to visit Shanghai is in its spring and autumn, when the _____ is neither too hot nor too cold.
4. Beijing, also known as _____, is the _____ city of China.

🔤 Language Focus

I. Here are some topics for small talks. Please match questions with answers.

Offering a drink:

( ) 1. Would you like some coffee? A. Thank you. I'd like a cup of coffee.
( ) 2. What would you like to drink? B. A cup of water is fine.
( ) 3. Let me get you something to drink. C. Yes, please. Black for me.

Travel:

( ) 1. Did you have a good journey? A. Everything went smoothly. Thank you.
( ) 2. How was your trip? B. Not so good. The traffic was terrible.
( ) 3. How was your flight? C. It wasn't good. I missed my connection.

Weather:

( ) 1. How do you find the weather here? A. It was cloudy/cold/windy.
( ) 2. How was the weather back home? B. It is lovely/warm/sunny.

Spare time:

( ) 1. What do you do in the evenings? A. I love watching blockbusters.
( ) 2. Do you like sports? B. Yes, I like sports very much.
( ) 3. Do you like watching films? C. I usually jog for half an hour.

II. Read the dialogues above with your partner.

Scenario Speaking

Work in pairs to complete the following task. Make a dialogue according to the directions.

Situation:

The assistant to the General Manager has picked up Mr. Williams, the potential customer, at the airport. They are now on the way to the company.

Roles:

Student A: the assistant

Student B: Mr. Williams

Requirements:

Make a small talk with each other. The following topics are for your reference:

1. trip;
2. weather;
3. city;
4. hobbies and interests;
5. food.

Workshop

Up till now, you have learnt sentence patterns and etiquette to greet others. Now it's time for you to work with your partners to discuss and dig out more non-verbal information about greetings and then deliver a one-minute presentation on tips of greeting others.

Some prompts are given as follows:

- body language (gesture, posture, facial expression, etc.)
- dress code (formal/informal, suit/casual clothes, etc.)
- taboos (family, politics, religion, etc.)

Self-evaluation Checklist

	Assessment criteria	Competent	Not yet competent
Part 1 Introducing yourself and others	1. Be able to gain the basic knowledge of making self-introduction		
	2. Be able to use proper sentence patterns to introduce yourself and others		
Part 2 Identifying yourself and others	1. Be able to talk about the factors and etiquette of identifying yourself and others		
	2. Be able to use sentence patterns to identify yourself and others		
Part 3 Making small talks	1. Be able to discuss preferred and taboo topics of small talks		
	2. Be able to use proper sentence patterns to exchange information		

Module 2 Understand Your Work

Unit 6   Meetings

Learning Objectives:

On successful completion of this unit, you will be able to:

- understand the goals of business visits;
- book a meeting through searching for specific information;
- arrange business meetings according to requirements;
- conduct conversations with visitors in a proper way.

> **meeting:** an occasion when people come together to discuss something or meet each other for a particular purpose such as business and entertainment

Part 1 Booking Meetings

📖 Reading

Read the information about Century Hotel and Park Hyatt and decide whether the following statements are True or False.

Century Hotel

Opened in 1998, it is 10 minutes' walk from the business and shopping districts. It is the first choice for many business people. There are two executive floors. They include 26 Horizon Club rooms, a conference centre and a business centre in addition to the hotel's main 24-hour business centre. Service is warm and efficient. Extensive leisure facilities can be found in the hotel.

Park Hyatt

The super-luxurious Park Hyatt is situated between the 79th and 93rd floors of a skyscraper in the city's most important business district. With 174 rooms and suites on offer, guests experience a true boutique hotel atmosphere. There are 15 executive floors. Recreation facilities include an outdoor pool, tennis and squash courts, and a fitness centre with fully equipped gym.

(   ) 1. Century Hotel is merely 5 minutes' drive from the business and shopping districts.

(   ) 2. The main business centre of Century Hotel is open 24 hours.

(   ) 3. There are no leisure facilities in Century Hotel.

(   ) 4. Park Hyatt is an economy hotel which is situated between the 79th and 93rd floors of a skyscraper in the city's most important business district.

(   ) 5. An indoor swimming pool can be found in Park Hyatt.

🎧 Listening

Situation: Jeff is the sales director of the company. Alex is Jeff's personal assistant. Tina is an employee from Human Resources Department. Jeff asked Alex to book a hotel to hold the annual meeting. Alex is asking Tina for some advice about finding a suitable hotel.

Listen to the conversation and complete the following table.

Hotel name	
Location	
Business facilities	
Recreation facilities	
Average cost	

🔤 Language Focus

I. **Study the following expressions for asking for and providing detailed information about hotels.**

1. Asking for details:

   a. Where is the hotel located?

   b. What's the service like?

   c. What are the business facilities like in the hotel?

   d. Is the hotel equipped for business travellers?

2. Providing information:

   a. The hotel is located ....

   b. The service is excellent ....

   c. A great number of business facilities, such as ... can be found in the hotel.

II. Work in pairs to complete the following task. Make a dialogue to ask for and provide detailed information about hotels by using the expressions above.

✏️ Scenario Writing

Suppose your boss asks you to book a meeting room at Century Hotel for the annual meeting of your company. Two hundred employees will attend the annual meeting on January 24. Write an email in 60-80 words to Century Hotel, asking for detailed information about the facilities, cost, transportation, etc.

You can use the following sentence patterns:

- We are looking for ....
- The provisional dates are ..., with ... people attending.
- We will need ....
- Could you let me know ... and send me ...?

Part 2　Arranging Meetings

Language Focus

Read the adjectives in the box to describe business meetings. Categorise them into positive and negative adjectives. Add more adjectives to each category.

| interesting | convivial | democratic | stressful | tiring |
| productive | disappointing | terrible | useful | fruitless |

Positive adjectives	Negative adjectives

Speaking

Complete the following dialogues with the adjectives from Language Focus of Part 2. Then read aloud the conversations with your partner. There may be more than one answer to each question.

1. — How was the conference?

    — We were very pleased. I think it was very _____.

2. — Was it a good meeting?

    — Yes, it was. All of us think the meeting was _____.

3. — Did you enjoy the weekly meeting?

    — We didn't produce anything new. It wasn't very _____.

4. — What was the meeting like?

    — We were under a lot of stress. It was too _____.

5. — What did you do at the meeting?
   — We discussed and determined the budget plan of next year. It was very _____.

📖 Reading

Read the following passage about how to arrange a business meeting and fill in each blank with no more than five words according to the context.

Business meetings are essential for effective planning, project management, interdepartmental coordination and staff oversight. When you arrange meetings, advance planning and attention to details help you make the maximum use of your time spent in business meetings.

If you are arranging a meeting that you will chair, be clear about what you want the meeting to accomplish. In any event, let participants know in advance what the meeting is all about and what you hope to accomplish.

Step 1 _____

If you are arranging a meeting for your boss or someone else, get as much clarity as you can regarding the purpose of the meeting so you can include that information in your communication.

Step 2 _____

You should not only lay out the agenda steps, such as introductions of the meeting participants, but also allocate a time slot for each step to help prevent the meeting from aimless wandering. Where appropriate, also identify a lead for each item. For example, an agenda might look like this:

Roundtable Introductions (5 minutes, everyone)

Quarterly Sales Performance (15 minutes, Jack)

Brainstorming New Marketing Opportunities (30 minutes, Cheryl)

Step 3 _____

There are often one or two key participants who must be at the meeting, so the schedule needs to work around their availability and itinerary. This can sometimes be managed semi-automatically through scheduling software in programs, such as Outlook, WeChat, etc., but not every organisation makes use of tools like these.

 Scenario Writing

Suppose your boss asks you to make an agenda of the annual meeting. Use the given template to create a meeting agenda. The agenda has to meet the following requirements.

Purpose	review department performance and determine what to renew next year
Procedure 1	review department performance to date and compare against benchmarks
Procedure 2	discuss whether missed benchmarks warrant a change
Procedure 3	discuss what to renew next year

Meeting Agenda

Meeting type
_____

Goal
_____
_____

Agenda
_____
_____
_____
_____
_____
_____
_____
_____

Part 3 Entertaining Visitors

🎧 Listening

Situation: Mr. Harris and Mrs. Wang are having a conversation.

I. Listen to the conversation and put a tick (√) next to the topics they have mentioned.

☐ A. The weather
☐ B. The journey
☐ C. The hotel
☐ D. Mr. Harris's business meeting
☐ E. Mrs. Wang's next business trip

II. Listen again and answer the following questions.

1. Why did Mr. Harris complain about his journey?
   _____

2. Why was Mr. Harris in London?
   _____

3. What is the purpose of Mrs. Wang's next business trip?
   _____

4. When will Mrs. Wang set off?
   _____

5. What does Mrs. Wang expect of her next business trip?
   _____

📖 Reading

Jane is preparing to welcome Helmut, a client from Germany, to London. Read Jane's email to Helmut and fill in each blank with a suitable word chosen from the box. Each word can be used only once.

palace	opera	pubs	attraction	cuisine
museum	exhibitions	concerts	bus	sightseeing

From: Jane@abc.com
To: Helmut@xyz.com
Subject: Visit

Hello Helmut,

About your visit next week, I'd like to show you around London after our meeting. Could you let me know if you're interested in any of these?

- Art (1) _____ at the Tate Gallery;
- Classical music (2) _____ or (3) _____ performance;
- (4) Buckingham _____, where the king and the royal family live;
- Famous tourist (5) _____, the London Eye;
- Trying our traditional (6) _____ such as fish and chips;
- Having a drink at one of our famous (7) _____;
- A (8) _____ tour of London on an open-top (9) _____;
- A visit to the British (10) _____ to explore the world's best collections of antiquities.

Please ring me on 24 January at around 10 a.m.

Looking forward to hearing from you.

Best wishes,
Jane

🔤 Language Focus

Study the following expressions for entertaining visitors. Then read the expressions aloud with your partner.

1. If you want to find out what your visitors like or prefer, you should use polite and friendly forms, such as:

    a. Would you like to …?

    b. Are you interested in …?

    c. What/How about …?

2. When you aim to give tips to your business clients, you say:

    a. I suggest/recommend ….

    b. I think … is a good choice.

 Scenario Speaking

Work in groups of three to four to complete the following task. Suppose your group plans to welcome a group of visitors from London to attend a meeting in Shanghai. You are required to give a mini-presentation about Shanghai to make recommendations to the visitors. You can use the format below to complete your presentation.

Places to visit:
1. _____
2. _____
3. _____

Food and drinks to try:
1. _____
2. _____
3. _____

Follow these steps to make your mini-presentation. You can also refer to the expressions in Language Focus of Part 3.

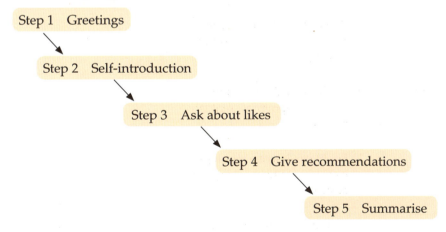

Workshop

I. Far from suffering "online conference fatigue", many employees have found the move to online meetings empowering. What do you think of online meetings? Do you think online meetings are better than offline meetings? Work in groups of three to four to exchange your opinions on online meetings. You can refer to the following table for prompts.

Advantages of online meetings	Advantages of offline meetings
• save money for business • easy access to communication • ...	• personal interactions with colleagues • free of technological difficulties • ...

II. **Classroom Debate:** Add more advantages of both online and offline meetings to the above tables and prepare for the classroom debate.

The requirements of the debate: Two teams are randomly selected to state their arguments for/against online meetings. The other students can play the role of judges. After the debate, to determine which team provides the most convincing arguments, a vote can be taken among judges.

Self-evaluation Checklist

	Assessment criteria	Competent	Not yet competent
Part 1 Booking meetings	1. Be able to understand how to choose a hotel for business meetings		
	2. Be able to make an enquiry by using appropriate sentence patterns		
Part 2 Arranging meetings	1. Be able to describe meetings by using positive and negative adjectives		
	2. Be able to use key information to write a meeting agenda		
Part 3 Entertaining visitors	1. Be able to ask about visitors' likes and give tips by using proper sentence patterns		
	2. Be able to entertain visitors by making appropriate plans		

Unit 7 Trade Fairs

Learning Objectives:

On successful completion of this unit, you will be able to:
- find out information about a trade fair;
- present products at a trade fair;
- identify the potential leads;
- write follow-up emails.

> **trade fair (US also trade show):** a large event at which companies show and sell their products and try to increase their business

Part 1 Preparing for a Trade Fair

📖 Reading

Work in pairs to complete the following tasks. Read the passage about trade fairs and discuss the following questions.

Every year many international trade fairs and exhibitions are held in different parts of the world related to different sectors. Here is some information about different trade shows.

The China International Import Expo (CIIE) covers technology, automobiles, equipment, medical instruments and medical care, service trade, food and agriculture. Enterprises from over 100 countries and regions are expected to participate in the CIIE every year. Supporting activities such as supply-demand matchmaking meetings, seminars and product releases will be held during the Expo.

The International Food & Drink Event (IFE) is the UK's largest and most important food and drink industry event, bringing food and drink suppliers from across the globe together with buyers and chefs from retailing, food service, manufacturing, wholesale and distribution.

China is the world's largest and fastest growing seafood market. More than 35,000 seafood professionals from around the globe visit the international trade fair, China Fisheries and Seafood Expo (CFSE), annually to forge relationships and expand their presence in this dynamic market.

Questions:

1. Why do companies prefer to attend trade fairs?
_____
_____

2. What do we need to prepare before attending a trade fair?
_____
_____
_____

Listening

Situation: Freddie is asked to book a booth for an international trade fair in Shanghai. He is calling the International Trade and Exhibition Centre.

Listen to the conversation and answer the following two questions.

1. Why does Freddie take a centre booth?

   _____

2. How will Freddie make the payment?

   _____

Language Focus

I. **Study the following phrases related to trade fairs.**

centre booth	pedestrian traffic	fit within someone's budget
transfer money	confirmation letter	Internet access
deposit	invoice	

II. **Make sentences with the words and phrases below. An example is provided for you.**

> Example: select/book a booth/when/lots of pedestrian traffic/.
>
> When you book a booth, you should select a booth with lots of pedestrian traffic.

1. booth/check whether/fits within your budget/.

   _____
   _____

2. invoice/after making payment/receive/.

   _____
   _____

3. when/confirmation letter/receive/reservation/?

   _____
   _____

4. online/can I/deposit/transfer money/?

   _____
   _____

 Scenario Speaking

Work in pairs to complete the following task. Make a dialogue according to the directions.

Situation:

Alan works in Shanghai Office of B. S. World Co., Ltd, an international marketing company. He is going to make a phone call to book a booth to attend the CIIE. Peter works at China International Import Expo Bureau. He is to answer the phone call from Alan by using the information in the box as references.

Roles:

Student A: Alan

Student B: Peter

> **Booth Booklet**
> Number of booth: 100
> Layout:
>   Centre: 40
>   Corner: 60
> Price:
>   Centre: RMB 1,500
>   Corner: RMB 500
> Facilities: Free Wi-Fi
> 10 percent discount for booking 3 or more booths

Requirements:

You may start your dialogue with:

Peter: This is Peter from CIIE Bureau. What can I do for you?

Alan: This is Alan from B. S. World Co., Ltd. I would like to book a booth at CIIE.

Peter: ...

Part 2 Presenting at a Fair

 Reading

Read the following advice for stand staff taken from a training website. Match the collocations in bold (1-7) with the definitions (A-G).

> ### Want to ensure success on your stand?
> Just remember these seven easy tips.
> 1. Always be ready to **make small talks** with visitors at your stand. It is a great way into a sales conversation.
> 2. Always **qualify potential sales leads**.
> 3. **Deal with** customer enquiries politely but quickly. You don't want to leave other potential customers waiting.

> 4. Be prepared to **overcome objections** from potential customers confidently and effectively.
> 5. Try to **get a firm commitment to buy** while the customer is at the stand. Don't wait until the follow-up letter or email.
> 6. Remember that events are a great opportunity to **gather customer data**. Decide how you're going to do this before the event.
> 7. And finally, try to **generate interest in your products or service** in any way that you can. That's what events are for, after all.

(   ) 1. make small talks   A. make people want to find out more about your product/service

(   ) 2. qualify potential sales leads   B. answer questions, respond to requests for information, etc.

(   ) 3. deal with   C. obtain a promise or guarantee that a customer will buy your product/service

(   ) 4. overcome objections   D. obtain information about customers

(   ) 5. get a firm commitment to buy   E. convince a person who has doubts about your product/service

(   ) 6. gather customer data   F. have polite and informal conversations

(   ) 7. generate interest in your products or service   G. decide how likely someone is to buy a product/service

 Listening

Situation: Steve, the sales representative for Compix, Inc., is presenting a new piece of Customer Relationship Management (CRM) software called iCustomer.

Listen to the presentation and put a tick (√) next to the features, advantages, and benefits of iCustomer that Steve has mentioned.

1. **Features**
   - ☐ iCustomer allows your customers to place orders directly with the company.
   - ☐ iCustomer provides a link between salespeople and customer data.
   - ☐ iCustomer provides a link between salespeople and suppliers.

2. **Advantages**
   - ☐ Salespeople always have current information about customers.

☐ It's cheap and easy to install.
☐ It's more user-friendly than any other system.

3. **Benefits**
☐ You will save money.
☐ You will produce a better product.
☐ Your sales force will be able to sell more products.

🔤 Language Focus

I. Match the phrases or sentences on the left with those on the right that serve the same purpose.

( ) 1. I want to tell you today about ....   A. First of all, I'll .... Next, I'll .... And finally, I'll ....

( ) 2. Firstly, I'll .... Then, I'll ....   B. Now let's look at ....

( ) 3. Moving onto my next point ....   C. My talk today is about ....

( ) 4. What are the advantages of ...?   D. Please feel free to ask questions.

( ) 5. In conclusion ....   E. To sum up ....

( ) 6. If anyone has any questions, I'd be happy to answer them.   F. That's a good question.

( ) 7. I'm pleased you asked that question.   G. Why is this better? Because ....

II. Complete the following presentation by using phrases or sentences from the above exercise.

(1) _____ Telesmart, a new communications package we're offering to our loyal customers. (2) _____ demonstrate how it works. (3) _____ outline the advantages compared to other packages available. (4) _____ show you how it can benefit your business, which means that you can combine all your business communications in one single package. It is much more straightforward than having a number of different providers for each service. (5) _____ how much money this can save every year ....

(6) _____, Telesmart is a convenient way of saving your money. Thank you for your time. Now over to you. (7) _____.

 Scenario Speaking

Work in pairs to complete the following tasks. Discuss a typical Chinese style product and complete the following table with the name, features, advantages, and benefits of the product. Then give a presentation about the product to the class. You can refer to the tips for presentation structure.

Name	Features	Advantages	Benefits

Three-step Presentation Structure

1. **Introduction:**
   Summarise what you are going to tell the audience.
2. **Main body:**
   Tell them the **features** of the product or service you want the audience to focus on, the **advantages** as well as the **benefits**.
3. **Conclusion:**
   Tell them what they should do next.

Part 3 Placing an Order

 Reading

Read the passage and match each phrase on the left with its correct definition on the right.

> If you've ever attended a trade show, you know that there are a lot of people and companies competing for attention. And you can stand there all day having casual conversations with people but never make a solid business connection, **let alone**

signing a deal.

That's why first you have to separate the good **prospects** from the bad ones. Then you have to make a connection with the good prospects and find out what they need. If you can manage that, then you're on your way to **closing a deal**. Closing a deal at a trade show requires a few **essential** steps. You need to show customers that you are listening to them, **build trust** and offer good solutions. Then you will be in a good position to ask the person to buy.

( ) 1. let alone   A. a person who is likely to be a potential customer

( ) 2. prospect   B. necessary or needed

( ) 3. close a deal   C. to create/develop trust

( ) 4. essential   D. to make a successful business arrangement with someone

( ) 5. build trust   E. to emphasize that something is more impossible than another thing

Listening

Situation: Tracy is visiting a furniture expo in Shanghai. She is trying to find a company there that can help her company with the redecoration of their showroom. She arrives at the booth of New Image Office Furniture. Dennis, the Sales Manager, greets her and tries to find out whether she is a qualified lead.

I. Listen to their conversation and fill in the missing information.

Tracy: As I said, we are hoping to update both the furniture and the decoration of our showroom.

Dennis: OK. And can you tell me (1) _____ that needs updating is?

Tracy: About 300 square metres.

Dennis: I see, and (2) _____ this project?

Tracy: Well, we are hoping to spend no more than $50,000.

Dennis: That sounds doable. And are you (3) _____ ?

Tracy: Yes. It's up to me to find the right company for the job.

Dennis: Great. And (4) _____ for this project?

II. Work in pairs to discuss whether Tracy is a qualified lead and why or why not.

🔤 Language Focus

I. For most of us, email is the most common form of business communication, so it is important to get it right. Although emails usually aren't as formal as letters, they still need to be professional to present a good image of you and your company. Below are 5 statements of steps to write an email. Put them in correct order (1-5).

_____	Begin with a greeting.
_____	Add your closing remarks.
_____	Thank the recipient.
_____	State your purpose.
_____	End with a closing.

II. Study the following expressions for writing an email and put them under the correct category.

Best regards

Cheers

Thank you for your patience and cooperation.

If you have any questions or concerns, don't hesitate to let me know.

I am writing to enquire about ....

Thank you for your prompt reply.

Dear Sir/Madam

Sincerely

I am writing in reference to ....

To whom it may concern

Thank you for contacting ABC Company.

Begin with a greeting	Add your closing remarks	Thank the recipient	State your purpose	End with a closing

✏️ Scenario Writing

Jessie Liu has had a discussion with her design team after coming back from the Gift Show. She is now writing a follow-up email to Jason Huang with the new catalogue as an attachment.

I. Discuss in groups and answer the questions.

1. How soon should a follow-up email be sent after an exhibition?
2. What is usually attached to the follow-up email?

II. Complete the email for Jessie.

To: Jason Huang
From: Jessie Liu
Subject: The new catalogue of products
Dear Mr. Huang,
It was a pleasure to meet you on the 17th of August at the Gift Show. Thank you for (1) _____. I hope you enjoyed your visit at our booth, and trust that your trip home was safe. I am writing to send you (2) _____ for the products you are interested in. Please feel free to contact me if (3) _____ _____.

The attachment is the new catalogue of our products for your reference. If you want to know more details, don't hesitate to let me know.

Looking forward to hearing from you.

Yours sincerely,

Jessie Liu

Workshop

Attending trade fairs is a useful way to promote a company's product. With the quick development of digital marketing, companies may consider investing in online marketing. What do you think about the changes?

Work in groups of three to four to discuss the pros and cons of online marketing, as well as the pros and cons of attending trade fairs. Draw a mind map to show the results of your discussion.

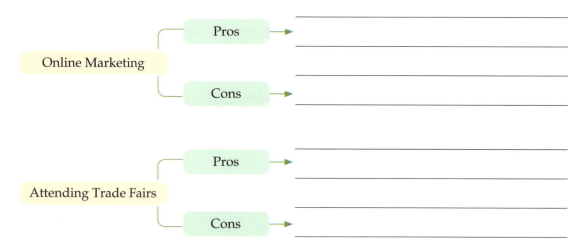

Self-evaluation Checklist

Assessment criteria		Competent	Not yet competent
Part 1 Finding out about a trade fair	1. Be able to tell the importance of attending a trade fair		
	2. Be able to book a booth		

(Continued)

Assessment criteria		Competent	Not yet competent
Part 2 **Presenting at a fair**	1. Be able to close a deal at a trade fair		
	2. Be able to make a presentation about a product at a trade fair		
Part 3 **Placing an order**	1. Be able to identify the potential leads		
	2. Be able to write a follow-up email		

Unit 8　Sales

Learning Objectives:

On successful completion of this unit, you will be able to:

- conduct market research;
- promote a product;
- understand unique selling points (USPs);
- compare traditional selling with online selling.

> **sale:** a transaction between two or more parties in which the seller exchanges tangible or intangible goods, services, or assets for money

Unit 8 Sales **85**

Part 1 Conducting Market Research

🎧 Listening

Situation: You have received a market survey on own-label products in the supermarket.

I. **Listen to the questions and put a tick (√) next to your answer to each question.**

Own-label Products Survey

Question 1
☐ government officer/teacher   ☐ company staff   ☐ individual operator
☐ housewife   ☐ student   ☐ others _____

Question 2
☐ junior/senior high school   ☐ technical/junior college
☐ bachelor   ☐ master and above   ☐ others _____

Question 3
☐ every three days   ☐ weekly   ☐ bi-weekly
☐ monthly   ☐ longer than one month

Question 4
☐ yes   ☐ no

Question 5
☐ yes   ☐ no

Question 6
☐ poor quality   ☐ poor packing design
☐ lack of awareness on these kinds of products

Question 7
☐ low price   ☐ good quality
☐ brand reputation   ☐ unique brand/product

Question 8

☐ service staff ☐ product layout ☐ brand image
☐ shopping environment ☐ product price
☐ others _____

Thanks for your support and cooperation.

II. **Have you ever conducted any market research? If so, talk about the experience.**

🔤 Language Focus

I. **When we conduct market research, we can use special questions to collect the information. Study the following expressions for collecting information.**

What is your job?

How often do you go shopping?

Have you ever heard of own-label products?

Have you ever bought any own-label products?

Why do you give up trying certain own-label products?

What are the main reasons that make you decide to buy certain own-label products?

II. **Can you think of more special questions to be used in conducting market research?**

_____
_____
_____

III. **Think and discuss the following question.**

If a supermarket wants to promote its own-label products, in what ways will it boost the sales?

Reading

I. Think and discuss the following questions.

1. Why must companies do market research before the launch of a new product?
2. What would be the bad results caused by a lack of market research?

II. Read the following article and choose the best answer to each question.

If a business wants to sell its products internationally, it had better do some market research first. Many large companies have learned a lesson from this.

Sometimes the problem is the name of the product. When General Motors introduced its American-born Chevy Nova into Latin America, it forgot the fact that Nova in Spanish means "It doesn't go". As a result, no one in Latin America would like to buy a car like Chevy Nova, which means "can't run".

Sometimes the slogan will also reduce the selling of the products. Pepsi-Cola Company knows this in its "Come alive with Pepsi!" campaign. The Pepsi campaign was greatly successful in the United States, and Pepsi translated the slogan for its international campaign. As it turned out, in German the slogan means "Come out of the grave".

Other times, the problem includes pictures and packaging. A smiling, round-faced baby has helped sell many jars of Gerber baby food. So, when Gerber marketed its products in Africa, it kept the picture of the baby on the jar. What Gerber didn't realise was that in many African countries, the picture on the jar shows what the jar has in it.

Questions:

(   ) 1. General Motors is a(n) _____ corporation.
        A. American
        B. Spanish
        C. German

(　　) 2. Which of the following statements is NOT true according to the passage?

　　A. Doing some market research is important in opening up the international market.

　　B. Nova in Chinese means "It doesn't go".

　　C. Pepsi was successful in marketing in the US.

(　　) 3. Which of the following statements is TRUE?

　　A. Chevy Nova was sold successfully in Latin America.

　　B. The Pepsi campaign was not successful in Germany.

　　C. Gerber sold its products in Africa successfully.

Scenario Speaking

Suppose you are the Marketing Manager in a large cosmetics company. Your company used to be a market leader in East Asia. However, your sales volume began to fall from 2022. You decide to create a market research questionnaire about your products and your brand. Work in pairs to discuss and write down the questions the questionnaire should include.

_____

_____

_____

_____

_____

Part 2　Making Promotions

Reading

I. Read the following passage and think about what USPs are.

　　For nearly every type of product there are many similar goods on the market. The unique selling points (USPs) of a product are the things that make it special and different from other similar products. A good advertisement, which brings the product to the public's attention, should describe these USPs.

　　The marketing department should have a customer profile in mind, i.e., the sort of people who will buy the product. When the department is trying to sell a product, it is important to give information about the product's features or characteristics and to emphasize the benefits or advantages of the product to customers.

Unit 8　Sales

II. Write down the names of the following products. Then think about what the USPs may be for these products.

	Product name	USPs

Language Focus

I. Study the following expressions for making enquiries and promotions.

1. Making enquiries:

   a. What kind of ... is best for me?

   b. Why do you think that one is better than the others?

   c. Do you have any samples with you?

   d. Can I have your catalogue?

   e. Can I have your price sheet?

2. Recommending products:

   a. This product is just right for your needs because ....

   b. The main attraction of this model is ....

   c. We strongly recommend this item for its fashionable design and good quality.

   d. This is a new arrival. Would you like to have a try?

   e. This is our latest product. It was launched last month.

3. Talking about prices:

   a. The price is very affordable.

   b. This model is very popular because of its competitive price.

   c. This is the lowest price. You know, our product is the best seller.

II. Look at the conversation below. Person B is promoting a car to Person A. Complete the conversation by referring to the sentences above.

1. A: What kind of car is best for me?

   B: _____.

2. A: Why do you think that one is better than the others?

   B: _____.

3. A: You mean it has a lower price than similar models?

   B: Yes. _____.

4. A: Can I have your catalogue?

   B: _____.

🎧 Listening

Situation: Karen Lee, who is from an advertising agency, is giving a lecture.

I. Listen to the lecture and fill in the table.

	What makes good advertising?
Change relationship	• To get (1) _____, the advertisement must make them think and look at the product in a (2) _____ and (3) _____ way. • The best advertisement can change the (4) _____ of readers, such as persuading them to choose a (5) _____.
Deliver (6) _____	• An advertisement that sets a real (7) _____ gets (8) _____ than those that don't. • The customers who identify themselves in a real scenario reflect on the (9) _____ and (10) _____ that they may get from it.

II. Listen to the lecture again and decide whether the following statements are True or False.

( ) 1. The speaker works in a university and is giving a lecture to her students.

( ) 2. Any advertisement can change the customer relationship with what is being advertised.

( ) 3. Advertising can show the advantages of a new product by influencing the audience.

( ) 4. Advertising is a method to support sales.

( ) 5. Advertising that fails to produce a sale is not good.

👥 Scenario Speaking

Work in pairs to complete the following task. Make a dialogue according to the directions.

Situation:

Your company is going to promote a new model of mobile phone. Two advertising designers are discussing what kind of advertising method should be adopted and who the potential customers will be.

Roles:

Student A: Advertising Designer, Tom

Student B: Advertising Designer, Sally

Requirements:

The following questions should be included in your dialogue:

1. What media should be used and why?
2. What message do you want to deliver in advertising?
3. Who would be the potential customers?
4. What is the budget in advertising?
5. When is the best time to advertise?

Reference hints:

Advertisement media: newspapers, radio, television, magazines, the Internet, outdoor bulletin board, billboard

Potential customers: 18-25 years old

Budget control: within ¥500,000

Part 3　Selling Online

📖 Reading

I. Warm-up: Think and discuss the following questions.

1. Do you buy products online? What are the advantages of shopping online?
2. Do you use any apps to shop online? If so, what are they?

II. Read the information about e-business and think about the reasons why it is more and more popular today.

> Electronic business or electronic commerce is a revolution which is sweeping across the world and changing the way we do business. More and more companies are looking for electronic commerce "solutions". Therefore, what exactly is electronic commerce?
>
> It is generally described as business transactions that take place by telecommunication networks, or a process of buying and selling products, services

and information over computer networks. The main channels of electronic commercial transactions remain the Internet and the World Wide Web.

Many potential benefits can be got from electronic commerce. However, businesses are not the only beneficiaries; consumers may also gain benefits using the Internet. They can receive an increased choice of products, convenience of shopping at home, and more competitive prices.

All in all, electronic commerce has demonstrated the great potentiality to be a very powerful business channel. Successful web-based strategies have already been carried out by many "traditional" businesses.

Language Focus

I. Underline the passive forms of verbs in the following sentences.

It is generally described as business transactions that take place by telecommunication networks.

Many potential benefits can be got from electronic commerce.

Successful web-based strategies have already been carried out by many "traditional" businesses.

II. Study passive forms of verbs.

Tense	Active	Passive
present simple	do/does	am/is/are done
present continuous	am/is/are doing	am/is/are being done
present perfect	have/has done	have/has been done
past simple	did	was/were done
future	will do	will be done
modal verbs	can do	can be done

III. Complete sentences 1-5 with the passive forms of the verbs in the brackets.

1. After a minute, you _____ and you can start using the Internet. (connect)
2. A lot of money _____ on online shopping every month. (spend)

3. All kinds of products _____ on the Internet. (sell)
4. More and more products can _____ through online shops. (buy)
5. There were more than 100 companies which _____ as online shops in 2018. (register)

Listening

Situation: Someone is introducing China's leading online payment solution.

I. Listen and decide whether the following statements are True or False.

(   ) 1. The expansion of PayPal into the Chinese market has been limited because of WeChat Pay.

(   ) 2. To Alipay, WeChat Pay is a forceful competitor.

(   ) 3. Alipay provides services like transferring money from one bank to another.

(   ) 4. Real-time payment means instantaneous receipt of money.

(   ) 5. If a user can't remember his or her payment password clearly, he or she can enter it up to three times.

(   ) 6. If a user's account is locked, he or she can never unlock the account again.

II. Listen to the passage again and fill in the blanks.

1. Nowadays, there are _____ people using online payment services.
2. Alipay overtook PayPal as the world's largest mobile payment platform in _____.
3. The Alipay app also provides services like _____ bills payment and so on.
4. One of the most important functions of Alipay is _____ payment.
5. An Alipay account requires the user to set up his or her own login password and a different _____ password.

Scenario Speaking

Some people dream of opening a brick-and-mortar store, while others prefer running an online shop.

Work in groups of three to four to make a comparison between traditional and online stores and complete the following table.

	Brick-and-mortar stores	Online shops
Opening budget		
Shopping environment		
Service		
Product price		
Method of payment		
Buying procedure		
Other features		
Your preference		

Module 2 Understand Your Work

🏛 Workshop

How can you sell the products successfully? Work in groups of three to four to complete the following tasks. Choose a product that you want to sell. Follow the steps below and try to sell the product successfully.

- Step 1: Draw a poster to make an advertisement including the following points.

Advertisement	➤ the size or colour of the product ➤ the function of the product ➤ the USPs of the product ➤ information about special offers

- Step 2: Prepare a promotional presentation by referring to the following expressions.

Beginning	Good morning/afternoon. Today I want to show you ....
The basic introduction	It is ... long/wide. It weighs .... We can use it to .... It has many colours ....
Special points	It is different from other similar goods because .... It really suits young people .... Now we have a special offer ....
Ending	Don't miss the chance. Just come and get it!

- Step 3: Invite questions from the audience and give reasonable answers.

📝 Self-evaluation Checklist

Assessment criteria		Competent	Not yet competent
Part 1 Conducting market research	1. Be able to understand the importance of market research		
	2. Be able to ask appropriate questions to conduct market research		

(Continued)

Assessment criteria		Competent	Not yet competent
Part 2 Making promotions	1. Be able to know USPs when selling a product		
	2. Be able to make comparison between different promotion media		
Part 3 Selling online	1. Be able to understand the advantages of electronic commerce		
	2. Be able to use passive voice		

Unit 9 Troubleshooting

Learning Objectives:

On successful completion of this unit, you will be able to:

- understand and complete a SWOT analysis;
- identify problems;
- make recommendations;
- deal with problems.

troubleshoot: to try to find the cause of a product or system not working correctly, and try to find the solution

Part 1 Finding out problems

📖 Reading

Read the passage about ABC Information Technology Group and complete the following table.

> ABC Information Technology Group is a company in developing, producing and selling computers. A number of years ago, due to some managerial problems, the company lost its reputation as one of the best in the field. Moreover, information technology business started to be very competitive. Many other companies were entering this market. Some of the customers switched to other companies to buy computers. Thus, the company needed a change. After several board meetings, the board decided to appoint a new Managing Director, Mr. Wong, who had over fifteen years of experience in the information technology industry.
>
> Mr. Wong's main task was to establish a new subsidiary aiming at providing services in the areas of support, management and maintenance. He also made a decision to cut unnecessary running costs to make the subsidiary more profitable. In addition, he stopped producing the products which were not making profits. After he took these actions, the company's turnover started to recover. The next few years saw the encouraging results. Now, ABC Information Technology Group is attracting more corporate customers, which means it is doing well financially.

Problem	
Solution	
Strategy	
Outcome	

🎧 Listening

Situation: SWOT analysis is a technique frequently used to assess the performance, competition, risk and potential of a company or an organization, a product line, an industry, etc.

Listen to the passage and fill in the missing information.

SWOT analysis is a framework used to _____ a company's competitive position and to develop _____ planning. SWOT analysis _____ internal and external factors, as well as current and future potential. SWOT stands for strengths, weaknesses, opportunities, and threats. Strengths describe the characteristics of a business or a team that give it an _____ over others in the industry. Weaknesses are the characteristics that place the firm at a _____ compared with others. Opportunities refer to the _____ to make greater profits in the market; external attractive factors which make a firm exist and develop. Threats mean the external elements in the environment that cause _____ for the business.

Scenario Speaking

I. Work in pairs to make a SWOT analysis for ABC Information Technology Group according to Part 1 Reading.

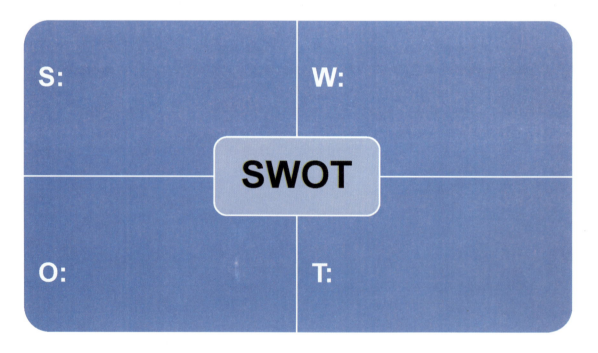

II. Compare the result of your SWOT analysis with a new partner. Are there any differences? If there are, why?

Unit 9   Troubleshooting

Part 2   Making Recommendations

 Listening

Situation: Two women are talking about the ways companies sell cars.

I. **Listen to their conversation and put the five topics they have discussed in the order (1-5) you hear them.**

_____ more women selling cars

_____ children's car seats and car phones

_____ soft sell from dealers

_____ car dealers and manufacturers taking women more seriously

_____ adverts containing product information

II. **Listen again and fill in the missing information.**

1. **Car dealers**
   - They _____ _____ us seriously.
   - They _____ _____ more women selling cars.
   - The dealers are nearly always men. I think they _____ _____ _____ a soft sell approach.

2. **Special Features**
   - Children's car seats and car phones _____ _____ available as standard.

3. **Advertisements**
   - They _____ _____ the advertisements, too.
   - I think there _____ _____ lots of product information in the advertisements.
   - They _____ _____ _____ us about things like petrol consumption.

Language Focus

Study the following expressions for asking for and making recommendations.

We use *ought to* and *should* to recommend changes or give advice.

> Example:
> You **ought to** hire a management consultant.
> They **should** listen to women's opinions.
> You **shouldn't** try to change the things you can't change.
> You **oughtn't to** postpone the meeting.
> What **should** we do?
> **Should** we change our code of practice?

Reading

Read the following sentences. Match each situation with a suitable recommendation.

Situations	Recommendations
(　) 1. We are losing our reputation as a first-class corporation.	A. We should try to offer something special and focus on excellent customer care.
(　) 2. Some of the products are not making money for our company.	B. The shareholders are very dissatisfied with this. We should ensure superior quality and good customer service to improve the situation quickly.
(　) 3. The costs of running the company are very high.	C. We ought to design new products to attract more customers.
(　) 4. The financial position is very weak.	D. We should think of ways of reducing them.
(　) 5. The information technology industry is very competitive.	E. We should appoint someone with a new strategy to make more profits.

Scenario Speaking

Work in pairs to complete the following task. Make a dialogue according to the directions.

Situation:

Amy works for a luxury goods company. She is now faced with the following problems:

1. Her customers are moving to her rivals due to their lower prices.
2. One of the staff is working until late every evening.
3. A new product is not selling well. She thinks its quality may not be good.

Unit 9   Troubleshooting   **105**

Simon is a consultant.

Roles:
Student A: Amy
Student B: Simon

Requirements:
Your dialogue should include the following contents:
1. Amy presents her situations;
2. Simon makes some recommendations.

Part 3   Solving Problems

 Listening

Situation: An interviewer is holding an interview with a manager about troubleshooting on large projects.

I. **Listen to the interview and put the following questions in the same order (1-5) as the interviewer has asked.**

_____	Do you have any other tips for solving problems?
_____	Are there any particular areas which are typical trouble spots?
_____	What's the most important strategy to avoid problems?
_____	Why do you think troubleshooting, or solving problems, is so important in business?
_____	Do you think that everyone has a role in troubleshooting and anticipating potential problems, or do you see it as only a managerial skill?

II. **Listen again and complete the manager's answers.**
1. Business is competitive in terms of _____ and _____.
2. Problems can _____ money and _____ time.
3. At the beginning of a project people often don't _____.
4. Planning helps to make sure that everybody _____
_____.

5. In a project everybody should make sure that they _____ and anticipate problems.

6. It's important that a project team _____ well.

7. You should try to have a _____ spirit in a project.

8. In order to avoid problems you should be _____ about the number of people working on the project, the _____ and the _____ of the project.

9. When you put pressure on a project, you _____.

🔤 Language Focus

I. Study the following expressions for stating the purpose of solving a problem.

Adverbial of purpose:

a. *to* do ...

b. *in order to* do .../ *so as to* do ...

c. *so that/ in order that* (+ subject + verb ...)

> Example:
>
> You should be realistic in the size of the project **to** avoid problems.
>
> The panel ought to exist **in order to** make sure that dealers take women car buyers seriously.
>
> Reports should be given to senior management **so that** they can propose a new strategy.

II. Match each recommendation with its purpose.

Recommendations	Purposes
( ) 1. We should open a new office in Guangzhou	A. ... in order to get help in making certain improvements.
( ) 2. We ought to hold a meeting	B. ... so that more women will buy its products.
( ) 3. We should invite the consultant	C. ... in order that I can anticipate any problems and try to prevent them.
( ) 4. The company ought to change its advertising	D. ... so that we can develop the market there.
( ) 5. I should plan for next year now	E. ... to discuss problems with the sales department.

Unit 9 Troubleshooting **107**

📖 Reading

I. Read the memorandum from Peter Shen, the Customer Service Assistant at a bank.

Memorandum

To: **Linda Lee**
From: **Peter Shen**

Date: **23/12/2023**
Subject: **Customer Service Questionnaire**

The findings of a recent survey of our customers show that customers are dissatisfied in the following areas:

- staff attitude (rude and uninterested);
- local managers (don't have enough authority);
- bank charges (very high);
- self-service machines (unreliable).

II. Work in pairs to complete the following tasks. Discuss the findings of the survey and put the four areas where customers are dissatisfied in descending order according to the priority for dealing with the problems.

✏️ Scenario Writing

Suppose you are Linda Lee at the bank mentioned above and you receive the memorandum. Write down some sentences about how you are going to solve these problems by making recommendations and stating purposes.

Example:

We <u>should cut bank charges</u> <u>so that customers don't switch banks</u>.
     (recommendations)   (purpose)

_____

_____

_____

_____

_____

🏛 Workshop

Work in groups of three to four to complete the following tasks. Do research on your group's favourite shoe company/soft drinks shop/clothes brand and use SWOT analysis to analyse the company's present situations.

You are required to:

- Work individually to fill in the following form. Please list 2 items for each aspect.
- Exchange your ideas with your group members to form the SWOT analysis of your own group.
- Report your group findings to the class.

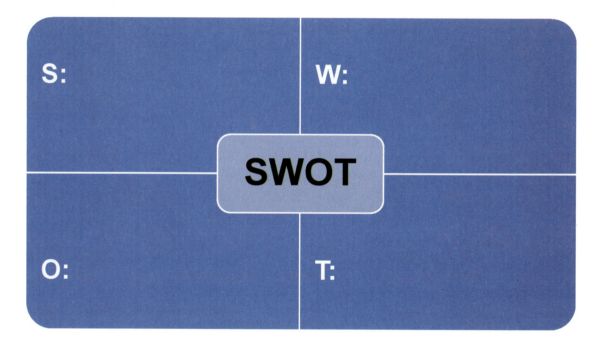

📋 Self-evaluation Checklist

Assessment criteria		Competent	Not yet competent
Part 1 Finding out problems	1. Be able to explain what SWOT analysis is		
	2. Be able to use SWOT analysis to find out problems in a company		

(Continued)

Assessment criteria		Competent	Not yet competent
Part 2 Making recommendations	1. Be able to list the modal verbs used for making recommendations		
	2. Be able to make recommendations		
Part 3 Solving problems	1. Be able to state the purpose of a recommendation		
	2. Be able to solve problems		

Unit 10　　Trends

Learning Objectives:

On successful completion of this unit, you will be able to:
- understand and read figures accurately;
- describe graphs properly;
- understand company's performance review;
- identify the fundamental elements of a business summary.

business trend: a general change in the way a business is developing

Part 1 Understanding Figures

📖 Reading

I. Study the three diagrams (A-C) below.

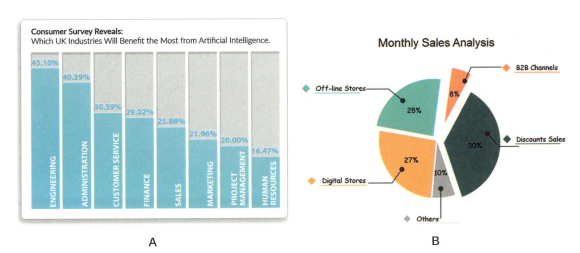

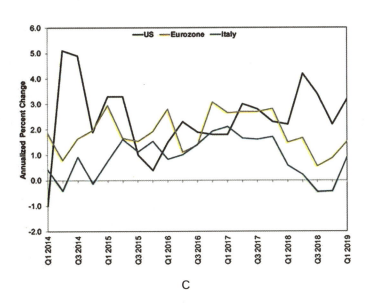

II. Match each chart (A-C) with the following chart names.

1. A •	• pie chart
2. B •	• line graph
3. C •	• bar chart

Module 3 Get to Know Management

🔤 Language Focus

Look at the five categories of numbers and choose a term from the box that describes each one.

cardinal numbers	fractions	decimals
ordinal numbers	percentages	

1. _____   0   15   30
2. _____   1st   2nd   3rd
3. _____   1/4   1/2   3/4
4. _____   0.25   0.50   0.75
5. _____   9%   18%   36%

👥 Speaking

I. Study the rules of reading numbers.

Dates:
For dates in spoken English, we always use ordinal numbers, e.g. **fourth** of May.
Order of dates and months when reading the date:
1. Month + Date: December 25th — used in the United States;
2. Date + Month: 25th December — used in most countries around the world.
Years are normally divided into two parts, the first two digits and the last two digits:
2017 is divided into 20 and 17, so you would say twenty seventeen.
There are two common ways of telling the time:
1. Hour + Minute (say the hour first and then the minute): 6:25: It's six twenty-five;
2. Minute + PAST/TO + Hour (say the minute first and then the hour): 2:55: It's five to three.
Way to read numbers in the thousands:
15,560 — fifteen thousand five hundred and sixty;
342,713 — three hundred and forty-two thousand seven hundred and thirteen.
Way to read numbers in the millions:
2,450,000 — two million four hundred and fifty thousand.

Unit 10 Trends

II. Look at the written forms of date, time and money. Work in pairs to read them.

24.10.2001   24.11.1975   31.3.1960

27.5.2010   25.6.1961

7:05   3:45   4:15   9:35   12:30

£100 $102   ¥1,000

€1,101   £5,000

¥1,000,000   ¥1,000,000,000

🎧 Listening

Situation: The following are sentences using figures to describe trends.

Listen to the sentences and fill in the blanks.

1. Sales of cars were _____ percent lower than last year in Europe.
2. At present, our greatest market is Asia, where we sell about _____ of our goods.
3. In North Holland, the number of cars sold remained _____.
4. The number of cars sold in Japan fell _____ percent to _____ units.
5. Sales of new phones in Southeast Asia increased to _____ units.

Part 2 Describing Graphs

📖 Reading

Read the text and decide whether the following statements are True or False.

The marketing world moves fast. Technology has changed the way we live and the way we promote and sell products. In the last ten years, increasing use of social media and online shopping platforms have allowed companies to connect with customers in new ways. The number of people who go online every day is still increasing, and the marketing trends we need to know about right now are digital. Here are two essential marketing trends that companies must take note of in order to move with the times.

1. Shopping on social media

It is reported that 72 percent of WeChat users have bought something when using the app and 70 percent of TikTok users use the platform to find new and interesting products. Companies can now create posts that allow users to shop directly on social media instead of companies' own websites. This allows retailers to reach their customers more quickly and easily.

2. Video content

According to Forbes, 91 percent of consumers say they prefer watching interactive and visual content to reading a traditional piece of information about a product. And consumers are 85 percent more likely to buy the product after watching a video about it. If an advertisement is interesting, amusing or unique, people will search for it online and share it with their friends. Live videos on social media platforms like WeChat and TikTok are also known to attract large audiences and get people interacting with companies in the comments, where they can give feedback and ask questions about the products.

(   ) 1. Television and newspaper advertisements are still the best ways to promote products.

(   ) 2. These days, people use social media more, shop online more and choose the videos they want to watch.

(   ) 3. Videos are a great way for companies to give information about their products and to interact with their customers.

(   ) 4. All of the TikTok users have shopped on the app.

Language Focus

I. Verbs and phrases in the box below describe trends. Put them under the correct headings.

rise	fall	increase	decrease	climb
drop	decline	remain stable	fluctuate	reach a peak

To make an upward movement	To make a downward movement	To reach the highest point	To stay at the same level	To go up and down continuously

II. Adjectives in the box below describe either the speed or the size of changes. Put them under the correct headings.

massive	sharp	insignificant	slow
gradual	tiny	rapid	huge

Speed of changes	Size of changes

III. Study the use of adjectives and adverbs in the following sentences.

Adjectives

There was a <u>sharp</u> / <u>slight</u> increase / decrease in sales.

Adverbs		
Sales	increased	sharply.
	decreased	slightly.

IV. Rewrite the following sentences.

Example:
There was a steady increase in the share price for the first four days.
The share price increased steadily for the first four days.

1. The share price rose dramatically at the end of the week.
   _____

2. There was a sharp fall in the share price on Friday.
   _____

3. The share price showed only slight fluctuations.
   _____

4. The share price dipped slightly on Wednesday.
   _____

🎧 Listening

Situation: Michael is describing Millennium Software's net sales.
Listen to the presentation and fill in the blanks.

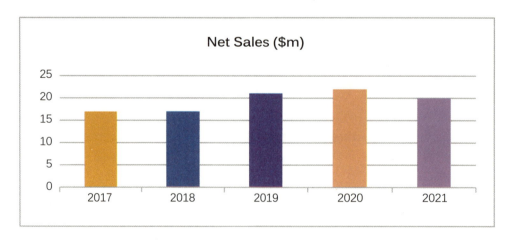

Net sales remained (1) _____ at $17m in 2017 and 2018, then rose (2) _____ in 2019 to reach $21m. This was followed by further growth as sales (3) _____ $22m in 2020. However, as a strong pound began to affect exports to Europe, net sales fell (4) _____ in 2021.

✏️ Scenario Writing

Write a short description of the graphs below. You may start as follows.

Smartphone ownership (percentage of population)

Smartphone ownership by age group: 2016 and 2021

The first chart illustrates the percentage of the population who owned a smartphone from 2016 to 2021, and the second breaks the percentages down by age for 2016 and 2021. _____

Part 3 Writing a Business Summary

Listening

Situation: The following is a presentation about a company's performance. Listen to the presentation and fill in the blanks.

Good afternoon everyone. Welcome to the presentation of the company's sales results in 2022. As you can see, this year (1) _____ very successful and the company (2) _____ all its targets for the year. Our sales people (3) _____ very hard and the department (4) _____ very well. The success is especially pleasing when you think back to the problems we (5) _____ in 2018. Back then, sales (6) _____ down by 40% and things (7) _____ good at all. Staff (8) _____ happy with the sales results. However, now we (9) _____ happy to say that our performance (10) _____ sharply.

Reading

Reports often summarise the performance of a company over a period of time. They can also be the results of market research and may offer recommendations. Read the following report on the performance of Eastern Ranger Hotel and choose the proper statement (A-E) to fill in each blank.

> The aim of this report is to summarise the annual performance of our Eastern Ranger Hotel in Leigh-on-Sea.
>
> **Profits and occupancy**
>
> Last year the hotel made a profit of just over £ 35,000, which was slightly under target. Room occupancy rates fell considerably after the summer season. (1) _____ Room occupancy in November, however, dropped to an average of 54%. (2) _____
>
> **Specific facilities**
>
> Facilities, such as the restaurant, bar and health club, are popular with guests, yet a large part of the clientele are from the local population, especially for the restaurant. (3) _____ The bar is also a popular venue for local office workers on weekdays in the evenings. (4) _____ The hotel has a well-equipped conference room but it is seriously underused.

Unit 10   Trends   119

> **Recommendations**
> We recommend that the hotel should target the events market by developing the conference facilities page of the website more, and possibly rebranding as a centre for training events. (5) _____

A. In the first three months of the year, on average, 67% of restaurant diners were not guests staying in the hotel.
B. These two facilities help to increase profits during the low season.
C. We should continue to build on the success of the restaurant by advertising it locally as a separate venue.
D. The most successful month was August when the hotel was running at full capacity.
E. Seasonal bookings resulted in only a slight improvement for December.

🔤 Language Focus

I. Study the following expressions for giving reasons.

Sales Profits	have	increased risen decreased fallen	because of due to as a result of	seasonal bookings. the success of the advertisement. the addition of two facilities. the well-equipped conference room.

II. Match the beginning of the sentences (1-6) to their ends (A-F).

(   ) 1. Production is more efficient ...   A. ... the advertising campaign.

(   ) 2. Distribution is more efficient ...   B. ... new packaging methods in the factory.

(   ) 3. Customer service has improved ...   C. ... the rationalization of management structures.

(   ) 4. Consumers have greater access to our products ...   D. ... our new centralised warehouse.

(   ) 5. Our market share has increased ...   E. ... new vending machines on all railway stations.

(   ) 6. A total of 450 employees have lost their jobs ...   F. ... our new distribution centre.

III. Complete the sentences (2-6) by using the expressions in Exercise I for giving reasons.

1. Production is more efficient *as a result of* new packaging methods in the factory.
2. _____
3. _____
4. _____
5. _____
6. _____

✏ Scenario Writing

I. Read this report on the performance of Laura Ashley, Inc. Underline all the phrases used to describe the relationship between causes and effects.

Company Report

The strong turnaround in Laura Ashley's results this year can be attributed to several factors. One of these was our new simplified management structure which led to faster decision-making processes and substantial cost reductions. A second factor was the increase in sales which resulted from new merchandizing techniques and greater employee involvement.

However, in North America our performance was disappointing. This was largely due to unsatisfactory margins, brought about by problems with stock control and distribution. We expect significant changes in next year's results.

Our new alliance with ABC Express will lead to better information systems and consequently an improvement in the flow of goods within our supply chain.

II. Write short notes in the empty boxes of the diagram below to show the chains of events.

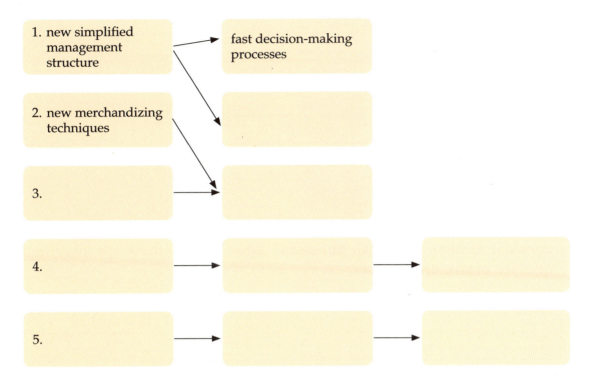

III. Read the passage below, discuss with your partner and think about other factors that may lead to poor sales. Use the above company report as a template to write a report on B. S. World Co., Ltd.

> B. S. World Co., Ltd specialises in selling traditional Chinese style products overseas. Their products are very popular among the Belt & Road countries such as Turkey, Thailand and Malaysia. However, the sales figures of the last quarter were not satisfying. The marketing and sales departments are having a meeting about the issue. They think that the pandemic is the main factor that affects the sales.

_____
_____
_____
_____
_____

🏛 Workshop

I. **Start-up companies are facing both challenges and difficulties. Would you consider running your own business? What do you think are important qualities of an entrepreneur?**

II. **Work in pairs to complete the following tasks. Discuss the pros and cons of being an entrepreneur and fill in the following mind map. Then make a presentation to the class with the help of the mind map. Some examples have been given below.**

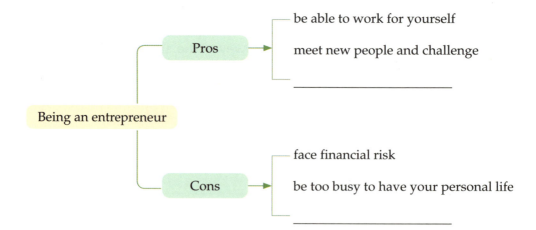

Self-evaluation Checklist

Assessment criteria		Competent	Not yet competent
Part 1 Understanding figures	1. Be able to identify different charts		
	2. Be able to read figures correctly		
Part 2 Describing graphs	1. Be able to describe changes appropriately		
	2. Be able to describe a graph correctly		
Part 3 Writing a business summary	1. Be able to understand the business summary of a company		
	2. Be able to write a brief summary of a company's annual performance		

Appendix

Listening Scripts

Unit 1

Part 1 Listening

1. Company A is one of the most famous brands in the world. It is the world's largest chain of hamburger restaurants with 31,000 eateries. The American company operates in 119 countries, serving 47 million customers a day. The company employs over 1.5 million people. The business began in 1940 when brothers Richard and Maurice opened their first restaurant. In 1948, they introduced the "Speedee Service System" which started the modern fast-food phenomenon. The golden arches trademark was introduced in 1962.

2. Company B is the largest auto company listed on China's A-share market. It is striving to get ahead of the industry's development trends, accelerate innovation and transformation, and grow from a traditional manufacturing enterprise into a comprehensive provider of auto products and mobility services. The Shanghai-based carmaker started its international business unit in 2011, and now has a presence in over 60 countries and regions. Its overseas sales network comprises over 750 dealerships.

3. Company C is a major American oil company that merged with another oil company in 1999. It operates petrol stations, carwashes, convenience stores and auto-repair shops throughout the world. It was founded in 1911 and quickly grew to be one of the world's most important oil companies. Its website claims: "This is the world's largest publicly traded international oil and gas company. We hold an industry-leading inventory of global oil and gas resources. We are the world's largest refiner and marketer of petroleum products". The company employs over 80,000 people worldwide.

Part 2 Listening

1. Xiaomi, founded in April, 2010, is a company which concentrates on smart software and electronic products. The logo of this brand looks like "MI", which is short for Mobile Internet. And it also means Mission Impossible which stands for overcoming impossible challenges. This company aims at lower price and higher cost performance. And because of this target, its products are accepted by the public so that it has developed quickly.

2. IKEA is a Swedish furniture and home decor retailer that has stores all over the world. It is famous for well-priced flat pack furniture that customers assemble at home. It also sells accessories and bathroom and kitchen items. It is the world's largest furniture retailer.

3. FedEx, or Federal Express, is an international logistics company. It began operations in 1973 and has grown to serve and reach every corner of the world. FedEx is regularly honoured as a top company to work for and is often on *Fortune* magazine's list of global most admired companies.

4. Heineken is one of the world's most popular brands of beer. It was established in 1864 in Amsterdam by Gerard Adriaan Heineken. He saw a market to introduce "beer culture" in Amsterdam's cafes. Today, Heineken is brewed by 40 breweries in 39 countries around the world.

5. BYD, founded in 1995, is a private high-tech enterprise. BYD has built nine production bases in different cities. The original business range of BYD was IT hardware, and it has engaged in automobile industry since 2003 and achieved successful growth. The success is fully thanks to the correct competitive and business strategy of automobile business and its successful implementation.

6. Since its launch in 1981, *China Daily* has grown to be the nation's leading English-language newspaper. In addition to its flagship edition in China, China Daily provides an International Edition in regions like North and South America, Europe, the Asia-Pacific and Africa ..., giving valuable insights into the second-largest economy in the world.

Part 3   Listening

1. Woman: Good morning! I'm Susan Peters, having an appointment with Miss Vetta in the Personnel Department at nine.
   Receptionist: Good morning! Let me check .... Yes, Mrs. Peters. Miss Vetta asked me to take you to the office. Personnel is on the first floor.
   Woman: The first floor.
   Receptionist: Yes, that's right.
   Woman: Thank you.

2. Man: Good afternoon. I've got a delivery for the Marketing Department.
   Receptionist: Oh, that looks heavy. Marketing is on the third floor. You can take the lift, if you'd like.

3. Woman: Excuse me, can you tell me how to get to Mr. Chang's office in the After-sales Department?

Receptionist: After-sales is on the second floor, but I think Mr. Chang is on holiday this week. Would you like to speak to his assistant?

Unit 2

Part 1   Listening (Dialogue)

Receptionist: Good morning. ABC Technologies Co. Ltd.

Caller: Hello, this is Stephanie Ferguson from XYZ Enterprises. Could I speak to Mr. Braun, please?

Receptionist: Is that Mr. Robert Brown or Mr. George Braun?

Caller: I'm not sure. I want to talk to someone about installing software.

Receptionist: Then you need to speak to George Braun. He's a software engineer. I'll transfer your call.

Braun: Hello, George Braun speaking ....

Part 1   Listening (Passage)

The majority of people in this country work in manufacturing, commerce and service sectors. A total of 11.5% are professional or technical workers; by that I mean people like accountants, engineers and lawyers. A further 7% are employed in administrative jobs. They are executives, managers, supervisors and so on. 15.5% of the workforce have clerical or office jobs. That's not only office clerks, but also secretaries, assistants and receptionists. Just over a third of all jobs are in production, 36% to be exact. The remaining 30% work in other fields, such as sales.

Part 1   Scenario Speaking

1. accountant
2. export
3. secretary
4. engineer
5. marketing

Part 2   Listening

1. Hi, everyone. I'm Caroline Green. I'm a management consultant. I give companies advice on their markets, organisation and processes. I interview clients, identify problems and suggest solutions.

2. My name is Jan Nowak. I'm a financial manager. My main responsibilities are to keep financial records, make sure the company pays its taxes by the deadlines and supervise how funds are used. I deal with financial paperwork, look after budgeting and plan any future investment.

3. Morning. My name's Kostas William. I'm a sales representative. I visit customers and leave product samples. I look for new customers, and I support my company's Customer Service Department.

4. Good morning. My name's Susan Ferguson. I'm a receptionist. I'm really the first person at visitors' first sights when they walk in through the door, so I have to look good, be polite and efficient, and pass them on to the right person. I answer the phone, issue visitors' passes, organise meeting rooms and make sure that mails and other messages are distributed correctly.

5. Hi. My name's Maria Salgado. I help to recruit new employees, keep staff records and reports, help to plan staff training, and organise team-building activities. I also participate in evaluating the performance of staff. Oh, I'm the human resources manager.

Part 3 Listening

1. Interviewer: Tell me something about your job, Nancy.
   Nancy: I'm an engineer for a big company based in Shanghai, China.
   Interviewer: Do you like your job?
   Nancy: Yes, I do. I deal with a lot of interesting projects, so I'm always learning something new. Our offices are located in the city centre. They are really beautiful. And all my colleagues are very friendly. What's more, I am paid quite well.
   Interviewer: Is there anything you don't like?
   Nancy: Well, I do work very long hours and have to work overtime at weekends frequently. Besides, I have to travel out of Shanghai quite often. I miss my kids. I wish I had more holidays — I'd even be willing to earn less money and have more holidays!

2. Interviewer: What do you do, John?
   John: Well, I'm a shift worker.
   Interviewer: So you work shifts?
   John: That's right, yes. One month I work from seven in the morning to seven in the evening, the next month from seven in the evening to seven in the morning.
   Interviewer: That must be terrible!
   John: Actually, I like it very much. I don't mind getting up early and I enjoy finishing at seven in the morning. I get a lot of holidays.
   Interviewer: That sounds wonderful! But is there anything you don't like about your job?

John: Well, the pay is not so good.

3. Interviewer: Tom, what do you do?

Tom: I'm an assistant. I work in the sales department.

Interviewer: And do you like your job?

Tom: Yes, I do. You see, I have a lot of contact with our clients, and I enjoy that. And I have a terrific boss.

Interviewer: Is there anything you don't like about your job?

Tom: Well, the journey's terrible. Sometimes the traffic jam causes me two hours to go to work. I wish I could have flextime like some of our sales representatives. I'd prefer to go to work early and go home early.

Unit 3

Part 1   Listening

Good morning, everyone. I'm very honoured to be here to tell you something about the FMCGs, which is fast-moving consumer goods and consumer durables.

What are fast-moving consumer goods?

Fast-moving consumer goods are products that sell quickly at relatively low cost. Nearly everyone in the world uses fast-moving consumer goods or FMCG every day. They are small things we can buy at a grocery store or supermarket, including milk, fruit and vegetables or toilet paper.

There is always a high demand for FMCGs. These goods go bad easily, like meat, dairy products and bakery products. They are usually sold in large quantities, with a shorter shelf life and high turnover.

However, FMCGs are the largest segment of consumer goods.

Now, let's see consumer durables.

Consumer durables are the consumer products that do not have to be bought often because they are made to be used for a long period of time (typically more than three years). They are also called durable goods or durables.

Durables have a long product life and are not worn out or consumed quickly when you use them. Since they're made to last, durable goods are typically more expensive than non-durable goods, which have to be purchased over and over again.

A washing machine is an example of durable goods — it takes many years and a long-time using to go bad. Moreover, it's relatively more expensive than other products.

Other examples of durable goods are automobiles, appliances, furniture, jewelry, consumer electronics and sporting goods.

Part 2   Listening

How do you contact your friends and families when you haven't seen them for long? Do you like to see their faces when telephoning them? Have a try with our new ViaTV Desktop Videophone.

It can be widely used for the office or for the home or for business trips as it's small and elegant.

You don't need a computer or any special software. It's very easy to set up and use. It's just like making a normal telephone call.

The ViaTV Desktop Videophone has many features. It has full colour motion video which means you can see the other person's gestures and changes of facial expression. It has excellent picture quality. With the adjustable picture setting you can change to sharp mode to get a wonderfully clear image. Thus, it is perfect to view designs or documents. The audio quality is also attractive to you, exactly the same as a normal telephone call.

What's more, the ViaTV Desktop Videophone also has a preview mode so that you can check what you look like before the other person sees you! And finally you would like the privacy mode. You can use it when video connection is not needed.

Now, of course, just as with any means of communication, don't forget to get one set for each party. A special offer is on at the moment, so now take time to buy the ViaTV Desktop Videophone. See both of you in the picture.

Part 3   Listening

A: Good morning. Can I help you with anything?

B: Yes, I've been looking online a bit. And I just want to know a few things about the watch you launched recently.

A: Sure. What would you like to know?

B: What's the difference between the Model A and the Model B?

A: Well, with the Model B, it's larger, and it has more functions.

B: Oh, how much do they cost?

A: The newer one, Model B is a bit more expensive, at 1,288 yuan. Can you hold on a minute, I'll go and check that .... Hello, we offer it at a discount of 10% off. The other one is cheaper at 899 yuan with no discount.

B: That's a big price difference. Well, what about the features the newer one has?

A: Well, the whole point is that it can be a storage disc to store files. It's also waterproof. You can take it up to 10 metres underwater and so on.

B: I see. And what sort of warranty do you offer on them? Is it a one-year warranty?

A: Yes, it is. Twelve months from the date of purchase.

B: Good. And could you tell me something about the service? Do you offer on-site service?

A: Yes, we do. It's free for the length of the warranty. And then 120 yuan a year after that.

B: And what about other guarantees?

A: Well, there's a 14-day money-back guarantee if you're not satisfied with them.

B: And what about delivery? How soon can you deliver them to my office?

A: Well, we usually have the Model A in stock, but I'm afraid the Model B is out of stock now. We could let you have it at the end of the month.

A: Oh. Well, I think I will go with the Model B then.

Unit 4

Part 2   Listening (Dialogue 1)

1. Secretary: Good morning. RTA, Lisa speaking. How may I help you?

   Customer: Hello. Erm, I have an appointment with David Barnes on Tuesday, but I'm afraid I can't make it then. Would it be possible to change it?

   Secretary: Just one moment. Yes, I can give you an earlier appointment, if you like.

   Customer: Yes, that would be very helpful. Thank you.

2. Secretary: Mr. Smith will be with you in a minute. Would you like to take a seat?

   Customer: Thank you.

   Secretary: Would you like a cup of coffee?

   Customer: Thank you very much. That would be very nice. Black, no sugar please.

3. Secretary: Shall I call a taxi for you?

   Customer: That's very kind of you, but I think I'll walk and get some exercise.

Part 2   Listening (Dialogue 2)

Kevin: Kevin Smith.

Sarah: Hello, Kevin. Sarah here.

Kevin: Hello, Sarah, how are you?

Sarah: Great. I'm looking forward to my trip to Shanghai.

Kevin: Good, we're looking forward to seeing you again.

Sarah: I just want to check some of the arrangements for the trip with Terry. Is he in?

Kevin: Sorry, he's out just now. Would you like me to take a message?

Sarah: Yes, please.

Kevin: OK then. You're arriving on Friday morning, aren't you?

Sarah: Yes. Friday at 11 a.m. I'll have a busy week at work in Shanghai, and most of my time is taken up with meetings, so I want to have a weekend to see the city.

Kevin: Do you want us to meet you at the airport?

Sarah: No. Don't worry. I can find my way to downtown area by bus from Shanghai Pudong International Airport.

Kevin: That would be great. Shall we book you a hotel?

Sarah: It's all right. I've already booked with the Palace Hotel. I stayed there last time and it was very nice.

Kevin: Well, would you like to meet us for dinner on Friday? Terry could reserve a table.

Sarah: Yes, that would be fine.

Kevin: Good. We'll pick you up at the hotel — Terry will leave you a message about the time.

Sarah: Oh thanks. One other thing — could you find out what's on in Shanghai that weekend? I'd like to take a tour and go to a concert or theatre.

Kevin: Of course. I'll ask Terry to send you some tourist information today.

Part 3 Listening

Helen Martin: Good morning. This is Helen Martin, Gree.

Susan Sun: Good morning. This is Susan Sun, High Technology. I'd like to speak to Mr. Pan in the Sales Department.

Helen Martin: Sorry, what was your name?

Susan Sun: Susan Sun.

Helen Martin: Right, Ms. Sun. I'll put you through to Mr. Pan.

Mr. Pan: Sales Department, Pan.

Susan Sun: My name's Susan Sun. I'm from High Technology. I'm phoning about our order for 10 air conditioners. We placed the order for TAE50 and TBC15 two months ago. The TAE50 arrived one week ago, but we haven't received the TBC15 yet.

Mr. Pan: Yeah, just a moment. Could I have the order number?

Susan Sun: Yes. Let me see. It's CEM1786.

Mr. Pan: CEM1786. I'll just check that.

Susan Sun: OK.

Mr. Pan: Yeah, I'm very sorry — we've had problems with our suppliers. We're still waiting for the delivery of some of the parts.

Susan Sun: Well, but our customer is waiting, too.

Mr. Pan: Look, I'll see what I can do.

Susan Sun: OK. But I need to know when we can expect delivery. I'll have to cancel if we don't receive it by the end of the week.

Mr. Pan: I'm very sorry again. Can I have your phone number and I'll get back to

Unit 5

Part 1   Listening

David: Hello, I'm David White. I'm a new club member here.

Lily: Hi. My name is Lily Collins, but please call me Lily.

David: OK. Where are you from, Lily?

Lily: I'm from America. How about you?

David: I'm from Mexico.

Lily: Oh, I love Mexico! It's really beautiful.

David: Thanks. So is America.

Part 1   Language Focus

Alice: Hello, Giovanni. Good to see you again. How are things?

Giovanni: Just fine. And you?

Alice: Oh, not too bad. Giovanni, do you know Brian Turner, our new Personnel Manager? Brian, this is Giovanni Toncini. He's from Italy. He works in Milan.

Brian: Pleased to meet you, Mr. Toncini.

Giovanni: Please, call me Giovanni.

Brian: And I'm Brian.

Alice: Have a seat, Giovanni.

Giovanni: Thank you.

Alice: How about some coffee, Giovanni?

Giovanni: Yes, please. Cream and sugar, please.

Part 2   Language Focus

Visitor: Is this Mr. Smith's office?

Receptionist: Yes, that's right. What can I do for you?

Visitor: I'd like to see Mr. Smith, but I haven't got an appointment, I'm afraid.

Receptionist: Mr. Smith is engaged at present. May I have your name, sir?

Visitor: My name is Sam Williams.

Receptionist: May I ask which company you come from?

Visitor: I come from ABC Company.

---

you as soon as possible?

Susan Sun: It's 6456 1536.

Mr. Pan: 6456 1536. Right, Ms. Sun. I'll see what I can do.

Receptionist: And is there anything particular you want to talk to Mr. Smith?

Visitor: Yes, I'd like to talk to him about a new product our firm has recently launched.

Receptionist: I'm sorry, Mr. Williams. I'm afraid Mr. Smith can't see you today. He's in a meeting at the moment. You can leave your business card here. Perhaps he can arrange a future appointment with you.

Visitor: All right. Thank you.

Receptionist: You are welcome.

Part 3   Listening

Small talk

1. The woman drinks black coffee.
2. The man's company is opening a branch office in Britain.
3. The little girl has started school and is in the second year now.
4. The little girl likes school. It's much more fun than staying at home.

Talks on cities

1. In the man's impression, the woman's city is clean, modern and beautiful.
2. The man really admires the city's long history and wonderful traditions.
3. The best time to visit Shanghai is in its spring and autumn, when the climate is neither too hot nor too cold.
4. Beijing, also known as Peking, is the capital city of China.

Unit 6

Part 1   Listening

Alex: Hi, Tina, have you heard that our annual meeting will be held next month?

Tina: Yes, I heard the news from Jeff. On the meeting he is expected to review our key performance indicator and announce this year's bonus, which is really exciting!

Alex: Jeff asked me to book a hotel for the annual meeting just now. Without any experience in choosing hotels, I am a little overwhelmed. Do you have any suggestions, Tina?

Tina: Oh, you are responsible for reserving the hotel for annual meeting. That's a big thing, and it takes efforts. Let's see, are there any restrictions?

Alex: Emm, budget is the priority. The total fees are set below $30,000.

Tina: That means the average cost cannot overtake $100.

Alex: Yes, the next thing to consider is the location. All of our colleagues are supposed to be able to get to the hotel by public transportation.

Tina: A convenient venue, maybe somewhere near the metro or bus station.

Alex: In addition to location, sufficient facilities for recreation and business are indispensable.

Tina: Business facilities? You mean meeting rooms, projector, computers and printers?

Alex: That's right.

Tina: OK. According to your description, Park Hyatt seems a suitable option.

Alex: What are the advantages of it? Could you introduce it?

Tina: Well, Park Hyatt is located in the financial centre, the centre of the downtown. The metro station is just 10 minutes' walk away. This business-friendly hotel has held over 200 conferences, providing facilities such as free high-speed Internet access, fax machines, printers and photocopies. Recreation facilities include an outdoor pool, tennis and squash courts.

Alex: That sounds like a luxurious hotel. I don't know if the costs are over budget.

Tina: Don't worry. Part Hyatt is celebrating its 10 years' anniversary. Discounted group price for over 100 people is $95 per person, which is within our budget.

Alex: That's great. Thank you for your recommendation. I will introduce it to Jeff next day.

Part 3   Listening

Wang: Hello, Mr. Harris.

Harris: Hello, Mrs. Wang, long time no see.

Wang: Nice to see you again! How are you doing?

Harris: Oh, not too bad, thanks.

Wang: And did you arrive this morning?

Harris: Yes, by train from London.

Wang: Did you have a good journey?

Harris: No, not really. The train was late and it was very crowded.

Wang: Oh, I'm sorry to hear that. Were you in London on business?

Harris: Yes, I was at a conference. Unfortunately, I didn't have time to look around the city. Next time, perhaps.

Wang: Yes. London is a very nice city.

Harris: How about you? Are you going on any trips?

Wang: Actually, I am going to Brussels to visit our new customer next month.

Harris: A trip to Brussels sounds great. There are a number of tourist attractions.

Wang: I plan to book the opera tickets in advance and go to the theatre at night.

Harris: A good chance to enjoy arts.

Unit 7

Part 1 Listening

Emma: This is the International Trade and Exhibition Centre. How can I help you?

Freddie: This is JK Trade Co. We would like to register for the 2021 Fabrics Expo. Can I reserve a booth?

Emma: Sure. Where do you want your booth to be located? Centre booths are more expensive than corner ones.

Freddie: I would like to get a booth with high pedestrian traffic. So how much would a centre booth cost?

Emma: It's 2,000 RMB for a 3-metre-by-3-metre booth. It's 10 percent off if you order more than two booths.

Freddie: Do you offer an "early booking" discount?

Emma: Yes. It's an extra 10 percent off. The deadline is tomorrow.

Freddie: Well, I'll take one centre booth then.

Emma: May I ask your name and your company's name?

Freddie: Freddie Pace. Our company's name is JK Trade Corporation.

Emma: Mr. Freddie Pace from JK Trade Corporation. Is that right?

Freddie: Yes. By the way, is Internet access available in the exhibition centre?

Emma: Yes, it is. We offer it for an additional ten dollars a day.

Freddie: Okay. That fits within our budget. What are the payment options?

Emma: You can log in to our official website and transfer money online using the reference number RF223.

Freddie: Is there a deposit for the booth?

Emma: Yes. A 200 yuan deposit needs to be paid within an hour. After paying, you'll get a confirmation letter and receipt invoice by email.

Part 2 Listening

Well, good afternoon, ladies and gentlemen. I'm Steve Dunn and today I want to tell you about Compix's new CRM application for your iPhone, the iCustomer.

Firstly, I'll demonstrate exactly what this software is capable of doing.

Then, I'll outline the advantages this has over conventional CRM systems.

Finally, I'll show you how this can help boost the productivity of your sales force significantly.

So, first of all, as a salesman I can tell you what we all want is up-to-the-minute information about our customers. ICustomer links your salespeople directly with your central customer database so that at any time they can check what exactly they want to know without any time lost. Moving on to my next point, what are the advantages of the real-time information provided by iCustomer over other CRM systems? Well, it means that for the first time ever your salespeople always have up-to-date details about your customers. Current credit ratings for example, any problems with recent orders or maybe a new special offer that headquarters wants ... of course, because it has a phone function. So, finally, what are the real benefits for your salespeople? Two words: increased productivity. Our research shows that salespeople are able to make at least 15 percent more customer visits per week, leading to an increased sales volume of up to 30 percent and that's not all.

In conclusion, if you commit to using iCustomer, we are offering a free consultancy service for your business. Our experts will visit your company and provide advice. Thank you for listening. If anyone has any questions. I'd be happy to answer them.

Part 3 Listening

Tracy: As I said, we are hoping to update both the furniture and the decoration of our showroom.

Dennis: OK. Can you tell me how many square metres the showroom is?

Tracy: About 300 square metres.

Dennis: I see, and what's the budget for this project?

Tracy: Well, we are hoping to spend no more than $50,000.

Dennis: That sounds doable. And are you in charge of this project?

Tracy: Yes. It's up to me to find the right company for the job.

Dennis: Great. And what's your timeline for this project?

Unit 8

Part 1 Listening

Question 1: What's your occupation?

Question 2: What is the highest level of education you have completed?

Question 3: How often do you go to the supermarket for shopping?

Question 4: Have you ever heard of own-label products?

Question 5: Have you ever bought any own-label products?

Question 6: Why do you give up trying certain own-label products?

Question 7: What are the main reasons that make you decide to buy certain own-label products?

Question 8: If a supermarket wants to promote its own-label products, which of the following ways will boost the sales?

Part 2 Listening

Good afternoon, everyone. This is Karen Lee from PDC Advertising Agency. Welcome to my lecture. Today's topic is "What makes good advertising".

A good advertisement changes the customer relationship with what is being advertised. To get customers' affection, the ad must make them think and look at the product in a new and different way. The best ad has the quality to change the mind of readers, whether to persuade them to choose a certain candidate or simply change to a different brand. This gives opportunities for the audience to be influenced, opening their minds for possibilities to accept new ideas, new products and services. Advertising that influences the audience can show the advantages of a new product.

Aside from changing customer relationship with the product, a good ad is clear in delivering the message to customers. An ad that sets a real scenario must get more audience attention than those that don't. The audience easily identify themselves by putting themselves in the same scenario. By identifying themselves with it, they reflect on the advantages and benefits that they may get from it.

All in all, the main idea is that marketing exists in support of sales. If the advertising is not producing a sale, it is a failure.

Part 3   Listening

Nowadays there are large numbers of people using online payment services. Of course services like PayPal have been around for years, but its expansion into the Chinese market has been limited. In China, it would seem that the online payment service, Alipay, has cornered the market.

Alipay overtook PayPal as the world's largest mobile payment platform in 2013. In the fourth quarter of 2016, Alipay had a 54% share of China's US $5.5 trillion mobile payment market, by far the largest in the world, although its share fell in 2015 as its rival, WeChat Pay, was rapidly catching up.

Alipay is used in smartphones with their wallet app. QR codes and payment codes are used for local in-store payments. The Alipay app also provides services like credit card bills payment, bank account management, inter-bank transfer, bus ticket purchase, train or plane ticket booking, food order, insurance selection, etc.

One of the most important functions of Alipay is real-time payment. For instance, when Chinese buyers make purchases in a foreign country, Alipay will deduct the amount of a payment from the buyer's Alipay account in real time in CNY and settle the payment to the merchant in a foreign currency.

Alipay provides multiple security mechanisms to make sure that user accounts are safe. An Alipay account requires the user to set up his or her own login password and a different payment password. The user can enter the login password up to five times and the payment password up to three times before the user is locked out of his or her account. To regain access to the account, the user has to contact Alipay, which can enhance the security of online transactions.

Unit 9

Part 1   Listening

SWOT analysis is a framework used to evaluate a company's competitive position and to develop strategic planning. SWOT analysis assesses internal and external factors, as well as current and future potential. SWOT stands for strengths, weaknesses, opportunities and threats. Strengths describe the characteristics of a business or a team that give it an advantage over others in the industry. Weaknesses are the characteristics that place the firm at a disadvantage compared with others. Opportunities refer to the chances to make greater profits in the market; external attractive factors which make a firm exist and develop. Threats mean the external elements in the environment that cause trouble for the business.

Part 2   Listening

Anna: I don't think car manufacturers and car dealers think about female customers at all.

Sarah: I know what you mean. Car dealers don't seem to listen to what women say they want.

Anna: Yes, they should take us seriously. After all, women are buying more cars these days.

Sarah: Yes, so they should have more women selling cars.

Anna: Mm. The dealers are nearly always men and they do such a hard sell. I think they ought to use a soft sell approach.

Sarah: I agree. I really don't like the hard sell. You know, I also think that things like children's car seats and car phones should be available as standard.

Anna: Yes, definitely. Why don't they install car phones in all new cars? Women on their own feel much safer with a phone in the car.

Sarah: And they should change the adverts, too, I think.

Anna: Yes, I think there should be lots of product information in the adverts. They ought to tell us about things like petrol consumption and safety features.

Sarah: I hate these adverts just showing us fast cars in exotic locations.

Anna: Me too.

Part 3   Listening

Interviewer: Why do you think troubleshooting or solving problems, is so important in business?

Manager: Well, these days business is extremely competitive in terms of time and money. Whenever a company tries to compete with another company, it tries to get a new project out quickly and it tries to do it without spending too much money. Problems, when they arise, cost money and

	they waste time.
Interviewer:	And, are there any particular areas which are typical trouble spots?
Manager:	Starting at the very beginning of a project, quite often people don't plan effectively. You can never plan early enough, especially in a large and complex project. Part of that planning involves making sure that everybody on the project understands his or her role, and that the objectives of the project are regularly reviewed, so that everybody understands how the project is going to meet the needs of the market and whether it is still relevant.
Interviewer:	And, do you think that, erm, everyone has a role in troubleshooting and anticipating potential problems or do you see it as only a managerial skill?
Manager:	I think it can quite often happen that managers start a project, think it's going very well, walk away from it and then are very surprised six months later when it's going wrong. Er, everybody, at whatever level, should make sure that they ask the right questions and indeed try to, as you say, anticipate problems and raise those problems with their managers and with their colleagues at regular review intervals.
Interviewer:	Do you have any other tips for solving problems?
Manager:	It's very important that a project team communicates well within itself and also to people outside the team. You should try to have a democratic spirit in a project, allowing people to speak openly, to ask questions and to feel that they own the project as much as the managers or the client may do.
Interviewer:	What's the most important strategy to avoid problems?
Manager:	In my opinion, in order to avoid problems happening you should be realistic. You should be realistic in the number of people working on the project, the cost of the project and the size of the project. When you put pressure on the project because you don't have enough people working on it, or you are spending too much money, you create problems. Pressure means problems, so to avoid problems, reduce the pressure.

Unit 10

Part 1   Listening

1. Sales of cars were two percent lower than last year in Europe.
2. At present, our greatest market is Asia, where we sell about 44% of our goods.
3. In North Holland, the number of cars sold remained unchanged.
4. The number of cars sold in Japan fell 15 percent to 8,600 units.
5. Sales of new phones in Southeast Asia increased to 10,700 units.

Part 2 Listening

Net sales remained steady at $17m in 2017 and 2018, then rose sharply in 2019 to reach $21m. This was followed by further growth as sales reached $22m in 2020. However, as a strong pound began to affect exports to Europe, net sales fell a little in 2021.

Part 3 Listening

Good afternoon, everyone. Welcome to the presentation of the company's sales results in 2022. As you can see, this year has been very successful and the company has already achieved all its targets for the year. Our sales people have been working very hard and the department has been performing very well. The success is especially pleasing when you think back to the problems we had in 2018. Back then, sales fell down by 40% and things didn't look good at all. Staff were not happy with the sales results. However, now we are happy to say that our performance has improved sharply.